The Day That Went Missing

Also by Richard Beard

Fiction
X20: A Novel of (Not) Smoking
Damascus
The Cartoonist
Dry Bones
Lazarus Is Dead
Acts of the Assassins

Nonfiction
Muddied Oafs: The Last Days of Rugger
Manly Pursuits (or How to Beat the Australians)
Becoming Drusilla

The Day That Went Missing

A FAMILY'S STORY

RICHARD BEARD

Little, Brown and Company
New York   Boston   Toronto

Little, Brown and Company
Hachette Book Group
1290 Avenue of the Americas, New York, NY 10104
littlebrown.com

First North American Edition: November 2018
Originally published in Great Britain by Harvill Secker, an imprint of Vintage, a division of Penguin Random House, April 2017

Little, Brown and Company is a division of Hachette Book Group, Inc. The Little, Brown name and logo are trademarks of Hachette Book Group, Inc.

The publisher is not responsible for websites (or their content) that are not owned by the publisher.

The Hachette Speakers Bureau provides a wide range of authors for speaking events. To find out more, go to www.hachettespeakersbureau.com or call (866) 376-6591.

ISBN 978-0-316-44538-2
LCCN 2018942130

10 9 8 7 6 5 4 3 2 1

LSC-C

Printed in the United States of America

Contents

1

What Will Survive

M ost days, on holiday in Cornwall, the family walks to the beach. A path drops steeply, and either side wheatlike heads of wild grass grow at waist height. Some of the seeds strip away neatly between childish fingers, and some do not. Each time I scatter a pinch of seeds into the greenery, I win. I made the right choice, and at the age of eleven it feels important to be right, or lucky.

We are a family from Swindon, England, on our summer holiday to the seaside. In 1978 this is what landlocked families do: spend a high-season fortnight on the coast, in Wales or Cornwall, in search of quality time that later looks bright and simple in photographs.

The family is Mum, Dad, and four boys. I am second in a declension that goes 13, 11, 9, 6. My brother Nicholas Beard is nine. For nearly forty years I haven't said his name, but in writing I immediately slip into the present tense, as if he's here, he's back. Writing can bring him to life.

On the sand at the wide Cornish beach we set up camp.

Mum lays out a blanket, while we tip plastic buckets and spades from a canvas bag. We take off our trainers, stuff socks inside. The picnic is in a wicker basket, and hopefully today's Tupperware contains hard-boiled eggs, my favorite.

The beach is huge, the sand compacted and brown. We sprint up and down, leaving crisply indented footprints, evidence that we exist with boyish mass and acceleration here, now, or verifiably just moments ago. Every year, wherever the holiday, we run faster—the prints lengthen and deepen, rows of four in races for a made-up podium.

In the sea, we jump the waves. Look, look out, here comes another. We cherish our special knowledge that every seventh wave will be bigger. We swear by our one and only fact about the rhythms of the sea, but rarely count to seven to check it's true. Some waves are suddenly huge, not thigh- or waist-height, but up to the chest, the neck. These are the best of waves, sent from the mysterious deep to amuse us. We don't go out farther than we can stand, and we're not interested in swimming. The fun is in the contest against wave after wave, whatever the Atlantic's got; we tumble for ages like apes, never feeling the cold.

At some point we'll dry off and try a game of cricket, but coastal winds blow the ball off-line and the bounce on sand is variable. The cricket never really takes because Dad wants everyone to bat, as if life is fair. He doesn't understand that we're in it to win it.

What do I know? I mean what I remember, what I carry with me.

One summer day in 1978, eleven years old, toward the end of a bright seaside afternoon, I left the broad stretch of beach with my brother Nicholas, aged nine. I don't remember why. Facing the sea, we ran to the right, away from the family camp, and clambered round or over some rocks. On the other side we found a fresh patch of unmarked sand. I see this place as a cove, with dark rocks close in on both sides, rising steeply to cliffs. The new sandy beach doesn't reach back very far.

The two of us are in the sea, jumping as the waves roll in. Until now I have tried not to know this and many times I've stopped, squeezed shut my eyes and closed the memory down. I can do that, crush it out of existence. All it costs me is the effort.

We were having fun, buffeted and breathless. I can believe I know this, even though the effort to forget has been immense. The memory is in ruins, but the foundations are traceable.

He was out of his depth. He wasn't and then he was. I can't remember everything, not each separate moment.

I don't know how, but suddenly he was out of his depth. I think I tried to push him back toward the shore, but the logistics are confused and I, too, am up to my neck. With my feet touching the sand my mouth is barely above the water. The instinct, because I'm not a good swimmer, is to walk back in but when I feel with my toes the sand sucks out from beneath me. The next time I try, only the tips of my toes touch solid ground. The ocean floor sweeps from

5

beneath me. Nicky is farther out into the sea than I am, and I don't know how that happened either. Is he?

His head is to my left as I look toward the horizon. I'm looking to him, away from land and safety, so I must be worried. He's farther out than me and too far to reach by walking, and anyway I'm in too deep to walk. I don't understand how he got there. I search with my foot for solid ground and my head is under and I just about touch and the sand rushes out. I push back up. His neck is stretched taut to keep his nose and mouth in the air, and he is panicked into a desperate doggy-paddle, getting nowhere. He whines, his head back, ligaments straining in his neck, his mouth in a tight line to keep out the seawater.

I couldn't reach him and I didn't want to go in deeper. I shouted at him not to stand. He had to swim. I shouted he shouldn't try to stand. He tried to put his foot down and his head went under.

Out of my depth, I was about to die. Nicky was trying to stand in water that was too deep, and in any case the undertow would drag him out. I decided to leave him. A conscious decision. I kicked my legs up and launched into a desperate crawl, face submerged, no breathing, a last resort to create forward momentum toward the shore. Front crawl was the fastest stroke over the shortest distance, though I didn't really know how to do it, and if I stopped to breathe I would die. I smashed my arms and hands into the water, head down, feet thrashing, because I understood that for me it was now or never.

Faster! Harder!

I understood with absolute clarity that I had one go at this. Run out of breath too soon and I would drown, exhausted and unable to find my footing. Keep going and I might get close enough in to stand, to live.

The memory is unsatisfactory. I experience the pain of remembering though I can't clearly remember. I was going to die so I decided to save myself, and staying alive took total concentration. I swam my frenzied approximate crawl until finally I had to breathe, and when my legs dropped down, my feet touched sand. The sand dragged me out, but I was far enough in to fight the undertow. I swam again, until I needed to breathe again. Chest-high in the water, waist-high, the sea was around my thighs and I could almost run, heaving my hips one way then the other, driving hard toward land, knees raised, escaping the water.

I don't remember looking back, or arriving at the camp on the main stretch of beach. I'm out of the water and running. I see a man. He is higher up, on rocks (or on a path above the rocks?). I tell him...I don't know what; whatever I said isn't part of what I know. I communicate the situation and the man stands up, gazes out to sea as if primed to make a decisive intervention. He takes off his sunglasses, and in a purposeful gesture hands them to the distressed and dripping boy.

I'm running again, to the right, over patches of hard sand between flat rocks, from one terrain to another. I remember looking down on myself, as if from above, running with the stranger's metal-framed sunglasses and finding them an absurd responsibility to have accepted. I throw his stupid sunglasses to the ground and they smash on hard rock and I don't care. I've broken an adult stranger's sunglasses, intentionally, and I don't care. I'm crying, I'm running. My face is out of control.

And that's about it. Of the incident itself, that's close to all I know.

My younger brother's name is Nicholas Beard. He was nine years old, and I was with him in the water when he drowned. Events that happened before and after are a blank to me. I don't know the name of the beach in Cornwall where he died or the date when the drowning took place. I'm not even certain of the month.

The general area is July or August 1978, the season of summer holidays, and 1978 because I was eleven. I can't remember everything and I can't erase everything, however fiercely I've tried. The scar left by that summer disfigures the age of eleven, and plenty more besides, but the month is obscured, the date lost to me. In nearly forty years, either alone or with my family, the anniversary of my younger brother's death has never been acknowledged or commemorated.

Which is an epic level of denial, because it can't be that difficult to pin down a date. The headstone at his grave will have it, but until now I haven't chosen to look. As it is, the older I get the harder it is to pretend that denial works as a strategy for sustaining inner peace. The memories I've wanted to suppress refuse to stay down, especially in stories I think I've invented.

Write what you know, they say. In my novel *Damascus* the main character Spencer Kelly is about twelve or thirteen when his sister Rachel, two years younger, dies in a car crash. More recently I've been closing in. *Lazarus Is Dead*, also a novel, provides the biblical character Lazarus with a younger brother called Amos. As teenage boys, the brothers go swimming in Lake Galilee. Amos drowns.

He didn't need to die, not in a fiction, but as early as primary school I learned in English Composition that the narrator can never die. If the narrator dies at the end of the story, how can he possibly tell it? I am alive and I get to tell the story. Only I haven't told it, not really. In the novel, Lazarus comes back to life and doesn't know what he owes, or what he should do with himself. Like him, I had a second chance. I write books. That's what I do, as if proving I'm the one who survived.

In which case, to write this story directly—without any fictional evasions—I should find out the date. It sounds easy, but I don't set out for the church and graveyard straight away. I have to free up an afternoon, which takes a while. One of the kitchen cupboards isn't closing properly and needs attention. I feel compelled to research emigration to Canada, then look into buying a narrow boat. Before setting out on a rash new writing project, of a type I've never before attempted, I should join a voluntary organization, or bite the skin just so off my fingertips. My teenage daughter invites me to debate the merit of piercings, at inconceivable length.

The trouble with denial, I realize, is that it makes life so damn busy. I should wash my mum's MX-5, which I'm borrowing, but the absence of the date nags away. It seems remiss to know so little when the death of a brother is a not insignificant life event.

I do have another memory of that day. Later on, in the darkening evening, in a gray house in a green Cornish valley (wherever this house might be), I went to bed. I am on the bottom bunk in a small room, and the room is at the end of a corridor. There are no carpets or soft furnishings in the house, only stone and wood.

I fall asleep, as at the end of a normal day. I wake up in the night, and I need to pee. I go out into the corridor, and Mum intercepts me on the way to the bathroom, or the way back. She wraps me in her motherly arms.

"It's all right," she says (though I'm inventing her words, after all this time), "you can't sleep—I understand that. Don't be frightened, or feel bad. It wasn't your fault."

But I'd been asleep. This is the memory I've chosen to shape and fix: on the night of my brother's drowning I went to sleep then later I woke up and I needed a pee. No drama. On the night her third son died my mum stayed wired and awake, so she misunderstood why I was up and about. She assumed I shared her sleepless grief. Because the banal truth would have made her unhappy, I let her believe I was feeling deeply, even if I was not.

Now, with age and delayed curiosity, I see other possible reasons for fixing such a moment in this cold and distant way. Already, on the night of the death, I had decided to pretend I was fine. Let Mum lose sleep and roam the corridors of the night. I felt nothing. I needed a pee. This is what I have convinced myself I remember, as if in truth children feel little, as if a death in the family creates less of a wound than people might think. Really, death is no big deal — adaptable little creatures, children.

I was an eleven-year-old telling myself stories. Nicky needed to be forgotten. I have persuaded myself that the drowning of a small boy who was also my brother, in front of my eyes only hours earlier, could barely disturb my sleep. Everything's fine, I don't feel bad. Mum just said I shouldn't, at night in the house with the words I've invented for her, though in the circumstances what else can she be expected to say?

"Don't be frightened. It's all right, my baby. Don't feel bad. It wasn't your fault."

Increasingly, though, I do feel bad, in a more general sense, and hate myself for pretending that everything is fine. At home, in my work, I've made a habit of looking away, as if a direct sight of life as it is might shatter me like glass. I create distractions by keeping busy, by writing fictions. The drowning set the pattern, an unwelcome reality I've chosen ever since to avoid.

I could get drunk. I don't get drunk. I'll fix the kitchen cupboard, but I already fixed it. Those voluntary organizations hum along just fine without me, and I don't have a clue about narrow boats. I want to find the missing emotional content in a lost true event, those feelings absent from my arch fictional glances at the edges of the incident. However late in the day, I want to conduct an inquest.

Nicky died, and the purpose of an inquest is to find out when, where, how, and in what circumstances. Once I have that information, in as much detail as possible, I want to believe that an intact memory will make itself known. The logistical and emotional truth of what happened may be held in storage in my brain; if I find the route to the correct door, the hidden closet, I can reveal what's inside.

A verifiable date of death is the place to start, with an inquest. I find a pen for taking notes at the churchyard, then lose it while I'm lacing my shoes, which means I can't leave the house. The car keys aren't in their place. Today isn't a good day of the week, or the right weather. I have an unlucky notebook, in a discouraging color. And anyway, Nicky's death and whatever I feel about it is unimportant. Nobody cares. It happened a long time ago.

My nine-year-old brother is buried in the graveyard of a Domesday church in Liddington, a village on the slope of the ancient Ridgeway in Wiltshire. Church Lane fills with the breeze off the side of the hill, high enough for views of Swindon a smudge on the plain below. Dandelions and buttercups yellow the green verge of the lane, while the petals of blown daffodils have shrunk into brown papery claws.

In the shelter of the lych-gate I'm reminded that young people die all the time. *In memory of the 8 fallen* 1914–1919 — *"In Proud and Grateful Memory."* This is how the young are supposed to pass away, for a reason. They are then commemorated at regular intervals, which is deemed right and proper, lest we forget. *Please*, reads the sign on the wooden gate, *No Artificial Flowers. Thank you.*

I could have chosen a better time, I think; there's always a better time. As it is, at about a quarter to five on a May afternoon this is where I am, outside an English country church beneath a canopy of high white cloud at the end of a sunny day. The church dates back to 1086, but centuries later a black-and-gold clock-face was added to the tower. The gilded hands have stopped at 10:31, but the rust on a metal downpipe is nature's more reliable measure of time passing. I lean into the wind blowing straight off the Ridgeway, buffeting the long grass beside the grave-yard path, punching the tough yellow heads of the buttercups.

I missed my brother's funeral. I wasn't invited. But I've attended five burials in the churchyard of All Saints Liddington since 1978, and on each of those occasions I could have checked the month and day on which Nicky died. The simple fact of the date is available, and factual confirmation will not break me apart. I don't think it will. Though I must have feared desperate suffering to have avoided his gravestone at the funerals of two of my grandparents, buried not far away, twenty meters at most. My dad is buried within touching distance, and his funeral was only a couple of years ago. Even last year I managed not to look, or not to memorize the information if I did, because my dad had a friend from the village who died; back to the churchyard I came, and left after tea and sandwiches none the wiser. Same again after my most recent visit, for a great-uncle I'd never met.

On these last two occasions I was making up the numbers, offering moral support to my mum. She shouldn't have to confront so much family sadness on her own, I thought, not in that church and that graveyard. Or such was the story I told myself as I knotted my funeral tie (black but with silver squares, to cut through the glum...). I've become my mother's funeral buddy. At short notice I will polish my black shoes to remember the dead at All Saints Liddington, where I'll carefully omit to visit my brother's grave.

Now, on a windy late afternoon in May, I'm here for this reason only. I will make a close study of the gravestone, though I'm in no obvious hurry.

I remember, I delay. My grandfather was once the churchwarden here. On Sunday mornings we'd pop a coin into his velvet collection bag, as if God were family. His was my favorite of the funerals, during a storm in 1995 with the priests dark against the hill, hoods up on their black robes, rain from the Dark Ages whipping in as the February light gave out. I have no mental picture of the weather for a funeral in July or August 1978, because I wasn't there. Where I was I have no idea, or if it was a better place to be.

After so many years I put off the moment a little longer. I realize I've forgotten his birthday. Sometime in March but this, surely, is the definition of ceasing to exist—in my mind my brother Nicholas has no date of birth and no date of death. He wasn't born and he didn't die; I have unhitched him from time, from his precise span of existence.

I've read every Church Notice in the porch, and should probably strike out for the boneyard. I ignore the path and take a direct route over unmown grass to the family plot, where the first stone is an unshaped reddish boulder for **Edward William Beard,** 1878–1982. This is my great-grandfather, a man I knew, and whose longevity features in *Guinness World Records.* He died four years after my brother, and I didn't go to that funeral, either, but the point of my great-grandfather is that Beards are designed to live (and work) forever.

Longest Working Career

Career	Holder (nationality)	Working Span	Years
Builder	Edward William Beard (UK)	1896–1981	85

Guinness World Records 2008, p. 120

The Beard family has internationally accredited genes for endurance, and historically we have exploited our super-powers to build extensions in Swindon.

A few meters behind my great-grandfather (104) is my brother (9). He has a rough gray Celtic cross, dappled with white lichen. Lichen is among the slowest-growing living things. And behind Nicky again, slightly to the left, is a gloss-white Celtic cross that Mum commissioned for Dad. Same stonemason, different results:

COLIN ANTHONY BEARD
29-12-1939–15-7-2011
ONE MORE STEP
IS ALWAYS POSSIBLE

The family motto is a recent invention, conjured up for Mum's tapestries of the family tree, which she updates every five years with names of the latest dogs and grand-children. Our disparate lives are stitched together by the ever-present motto, and its hopeful appeal to a common family purpose, or stubbornness. One More Step. Always possible, whether we like it or not.

Nicky's cross. I'm in the churchyard, lest I forget, to look properly at his unchanging gravestone. I can take a photo on my phone, and carry with me forever after the date I've blocked out so efficiently. But however I attempt to frame the lettering on the screen, my dad's headstone encroaches into the background. I narrow and then spread the focus, but some edge of Dad's white cross always intrudes. I take the photo anyway.

IN
LOVING MEMORY
NICHOLAS
PAUL
BEARD
1969–1978

His actual dates aren't recorded. Nicholas Paul Beard, in loving memory, exists as a floating notion between unfixed points in 1969 and 1978. I feel resentful on his behalf— not much love in a vague loving memory. He died on a particular date. No use denying it, yet even the gravestone omits the details. I hadn't noticed until now, and hadn't cared—I have truly not been paying attention.

Nicky has a second memorial, in addition to the stone. The last time I saw it was in 1984, because aged seventeen I took a girl I liked on a winter date to an empty school, and tramped round the deserted playing fields. We came upon the closed-up cricket scorebox, and I lingered there blowing on my fingers until she saw the plaque commemorating my brother, dead for the past five years.

Oh, poor me. Poor, poor me. By then I was indifferent to death, and also to broken hearts, because I'd enrolled dead Nicky into a strategy. The girl, beautiful and perplexed, would see the tragic plaque and feel sincere emotion on my behalf, which I fully intended to exploit. She'd appreciate me afresh for the silence of my suffering, then sleep with me to comfort or to save me, or out of pity. Any of these motivations was acceptable.

However cynical the use I was making of a sadly dead brother, the point is that my ploy at the scorebox is how I know there's another memorial in rural Berkshire. The plaque on the cricket-scorebox door will tell me the date.

Out of term-time, the main building at Pinewood School, at the end of a curved tree-lined drive, remains familiar. Pevsner gives the building a brief entry in *Buildings of England — Berkshire*: *Pinewood, formerly Bourton House, Tudor and gabled is by F. W. Ordish and the tender in* 1845 *was for £6,650.*

So the school, once a private house, was built in the early Victorian era to look Tudor. Nothing here is quite as it seems. In the 1970s, for example, we experienced a style of education from at least twenty years earlier. The headmaster, Geoffrey "Goat" Walters, had started as a Pinewood teacher in 1942.

According to the 1975 prospectus, Pinewood had "a complement of 100 pupils and a staff of 9," and the brochure met the main cause of parental worry about boarding schools head-on: *Of course he may experience the odd bout of homesickness initially, but this is perfectly natural. Boys quickly settle down.* Numbers were dwindling, possibly because parents in the Seventies wanted more for their children than the frigid settling down of the Fifties. Social expectations were changing, and emotional sensitivity had its place in a rounded education.

Vladimir Nabokov, a novelist with a taste for memoir, wrote that everyone is at home in their past. He never went to an English boarding school. I'm at school in my past, and on a sunny day, more than thirty years after I left, during summer half-term I was greeted at the school's main double doorway, implausibly, by a music teacher who'd once taught me piano. Mr. Field arrived at Pinewood in 1977. Now his job was mostly to charm visitors like me. Or not like me, because my reason for being here was unlike anyone else's. I could still see the younger Mr. Field in the man he'd become, and after some initial pleasantries, I hoped he might be able to help.

"What do you remember about Nicky?"

He remembered Nicky as dead. No one was going to forget that, but of the living schoolboy he recalled a mood rather than details.

"He was unsettled. He was a boy who didn't settle well."

I interpreted this as schoolmaster code for a boy racked with grief when his parents abandoned him, but that was unfair. I was moving too fast, too soon. I should find out the date of his death before making guesses about his character.

Mr. Field offered a tour of the school, and I couldn't resist, but inside the old building so much had changed that the place was barely recognizable. Classrooms had been reconfigured with false walls, and connected by rerouted corridors like pathways in a new brain, one that didn't make sense to me. Upstairs, I followed Mr. Field through the dormitories, but the corners and squat sit-on radiators had gone, the places where boys used to cry. I, too, had my moments of not settling well.

They didn't last long. Sport, friendship, and routine would take over, and back inside these walls memories of gray shorts and sweaters brush against me, but no more than that: I feel a trace of sensation from older stonework, a glimmer of my past life in a wall of faded tiling I'd have seen day in, day out, so many years ago. I stop at a wooden stairwell, each step worn and discolored by the tread of buckled brown sandals. At the top stair the wooden banister is smooth from the touch of a thousand small hands, and I'm a boy in an Aertex shirt filing down from the dormitories to breakfast. One among many. I hear days soundtracked by tunes from Grade 2 exam books, the music played without sufficient expression.

We leave through the back of the house and walk down a steep grass bank to the playing fields. Nicky's memorial scorebox used to be on the far side of the First XI cricket pitch, but now the scorebox is off to the right, beside a new pavilion. The box is unlocked so I search inside and out. No sign of a plaque. I take some photos anyway, from a sense of obligation, before realizing one cricket scorebox looks much like another. I spy a similar black box at the farthest corner of the fields, close against a barbed-wire fence between the grounds and farmland.

Mr. Field is getting old now, so I make the trek alone.

The second scorebox is being used as a groundsman's shed, and the outside has been protected several times over with layers of clumsy black creosote. A small brass plaque is screwed to the door, the edges overpainted:

THIS SCOREBOARD WAS PRESENTED TO THE SCHOOL
BY MEMBERS AND FRIENDS OF THE BEARD FAMILY
IN MEMORY OF NICHOLAS
(PINEWOOD 1977–1978)

Again, no date. And here Nicholas Beard is remembered as having only a single meaningful year of life: *Pinewood 1977–1978*. He had more to him than that, I'm sure of it, but at least the memorial exists, albeit at the very edge of school property and no longer keeping the score for the *members and friends of the Beard family.*

I consider stealing the plaque, because soon this box is going to be useless even for storage. Whoever chose the memorial must have known the gesture wouldn't last— wooden cricket scoreboxes don't become listed buildings. Though judging by our talent for forgetting, a perishable monument may have been part of the attraction. The school chapel was also available if we'd wanted something more permanent.

The chapel has gone, converted into an extension of the

primary-school staffroom and an extra classroom. Scribbled infant pictures cover the wall where the hymn numbers used to hang. In place of the wooden-eagle lectern, the classroom has beanbags. All that remains of the building's past is an annex: the former entrance to the chapel preserved as a "lady chapel." This is a tiny space, an awkward, durable portion of the past. The old school altarware is kept here, along with a wooden plaque carved with a cross:

In Memory of Nicholas Beard Summer 1978.

"Summer." His life gets shorter with each memorial, until he's remembered in a permanent season of sunshine. Not good enough, for an inquest. Nicky died on a specific numbered day, the date I still don't have.

Mum will know. I presume the dead boy's mother will remember the date he died, so I phone ahead to warn her I'm coming. I don't say why, but aim the Mazda across out-of-town roundabouts into Swindon itself, and then toward Mum's new bungalow, which isn't that new anymore. We grew up in a house in the next street, and by car I feel like I'm going to the same place, until at the last minute I'm not.

Dad died in the main bedroom here, and now it's just my mum; her territory, her rules. In the lounge I hold back the big question, because first we have to set up camp, make our safe and central place. Tea, biscuits, the tray on a table between sofas. We sit at right angles to each other, with the dogs in baskets by the television. Mum waits. She knows I want something, and I hesitate to describe my own mum as she sits on a sofa while the tea brews. She looks at the dogs, at the squirrels out the window, but in the end mums are like anyone else. They get older as you get older, and they have problems too. More importantly, mums are there from the beginning. They were there.

I eat a chocolate biscuit, then another. I'm stuck for an opening line because I've spent so many years not asking this question. The gold carriage clock above the fireplace goes tick-tock, an engraved present to my dad's parents for their golden wedding (1931–1981). The names of their children and grandchildren are engraved on the sides and back of the pedestal. Nicky's name is absent, unrecorded, nonexistent.

I tell Mum I'm having trouble at home. I realize I'm preparing the terrain, casting myself as a serious individual with serious concerns. I have troubles. I'm an adult, married but at the next stage beyond even that, with a marriage in danger of failing. In other words, I'm in the mood for straightening stuff out.

"I've been behaving strangely," I say. "I'm not feeling emotions very deeply."

"You have such wonderful children," Mum says, choosing the road more traveled. She is on solid ground here, and we recognize the scenery of a familiar conversation. We know where we are with biscuits and the wonderful children.

"Mum. I have a couple of things I'd like to chat about."

What I mean is we have an annex to our lives that as a

family we pretend isn't there. If I can enter that neglected space, I might discover why I increasingly feel that life is empty and worthless.

But old habits die hard. My default strategy for avoiding these memories is to allow stories to take their place. For the sake of the story, a narrative interdiction here would be perfect. I'll explain my inquest into Nicky's death, but Mum will insist there's nothing special to know. You're wasting your time, she'll say. She'll warn me off, and threaten to talk to my brothers, while hinting darkly at disinheritance. To create tension, she should raise the narrative stakes.

"I want to talk about Nicky's death."

Mum talks. No interdiction, no problem. She has wanted to open up about Nicky for years, she says, and barely knows where to start. At the butcher's, as it happens, that's where her mind goes first. One of the hardest times, she tells me, was after Nicky died and back from our holiday in Cornwall Mum forced herself out to the shops, to Eastcott Smith in Wood Street.

"Five lamb chops," she said, hating the sound of the number. "Five chops, please."

Five, not six. The lamb-chop moment, the first time she came home from the shops without any dinner for Nicky, almost broke her heart.

But I've heard it, know it. The trip to Eastcott Smith's for five lamb chops is the one allowed story, which doesn't make it any less true or sad. More likely, I think, is that this single domestic memory stands in for every sudden grief, large or small, that has since been denied or suppressed. The denial started early.

"Mum, I don't know the date."

"August the eighteenth," she says.

18th August 1978—fact. Finally, I have the date.

The fact itself, the specific information, doesn't break me. I check but no, I'm not falling apart. The inquest has begun and the past can be pulled back into being, even if during the years since 18th August 1978, until about yesterday, Mum kept Nicky alive by telling her story about chops. Occasionally she would say his name. Not often, but conspicuously enough for us to recognize the vacuum of silence that always followed. She made sure his black-and-white photo was on the piano, that he had his place beside the color-fast grandchildren.

"I always talked about him," she says, but I remember the photo appearing on the piano after a certain amount of time had passed, measurable in years. Maybe at first I avoided noticing the photo, but I don't think so.

"He was a difficult child," Mum says, "a naughty child. He was either going to be a banker or a murderer."

Why would Mum say that? I don't know what she's saying.

"He wasn't like you," she goes on, unstoppable now. "He was hopeless at games, and not very brainy. At cricket he tried, but he was out first ball. I'd go to watch his match, and he'd drop a catch."

Which might help explain why he died. He wasn't physically competent. He didn't have the muscle coordination to fight back against the water. Though mostly he was young, so very young. Nine years old in a battle with the Atlantic.

"He looked completely different to you three," Mum says, "huge brown eyes and thin black hair."

I let a pause develop, because I can be unkind. It is one of the symptoms of being insufficient in feeling. Nicky looked physically different from his three brothers, and according to Mum was unlike us in his talents and temperament. Which could account for his death being erased from the family memory. He wasn't genuinely one of us — a reason for forgetting him that would make sense, in a novel.

"Your dad was definitely his father," my mum says, understanding exactly what my pause is designed to suggest. "You can be sure of that."

We've departed solid ground for the uncertain past, but out of habit we look for a safe way back. I can be unkind but I prefer to be comfortable, and this has been true for as long as I remember.

"It's good to talk," I say, more as an attempt at appeasement than because I honestly believe it. "Get these things out in the open."

We've shut away so much. After all this time I have a miserable lack of factual information. Off the top of my head I'd say we have eleven, maybe twelve photographs, in total, that survive of Nicky. Roughly half are Nicky in a family group in the back garden of my grandparents' house. My Swindon grandfather was a keen photographer, with his own darkroom (top of the stairs, turn right). At least twice a year he'd pose the four of us boys on the steps beside the rock garden. The steps stayed the same while the children aged and grew.

Otherwise I knew of a few holiday snaps, and a couple of photos of Nicky playing cricket, as well as the statement picture on the piano. Inside his special silver frame, Nicky on the piano in black and white is none too real. He sits on a gray grass bank in his summer school uniform, perfect for the shot because everything he wears is gray, his socks, shorts, shirt, sweater. Physically Nicky is a thin boy, wiry, a string bean. He has black hair and brown eyes, and in the photo this is what he does: he sits on a grass bank with his legs crossed at the ankle.

I can't find him, not fully, in this photograph. I can't *feel* him. I've never consciously preserved memories of how he was as a person, because my brain has been used up suppressing the more aggressive memory of the two of us in the water. That left no space either for Nicky as the person he was before, or for what became of him afterward. Oh, my poor old mum, I think, and on I charge.

"Did they ever find the body?"

Not much of an inquest without a body, though with drowning the body can be a source of complications. The sodden corpse can be seized by currents and lost at sea.

Fish peck at softened flesh until the bones separate and sink into the Atlantic darkness. The exhausted bone matter flakes into sand, and random particles formerly known as Nicholas Beard diffuse across the oceans and wash up on shores. He exists, but is dispersed and untraceable.

In 1978 at an ancient churchyard in an English village, led by an Anglican vicar with his Book of Common Prayer, my parents may have buried an empty box. *Lord, have mercy upon us.* Better than nothing. The memorial gift to the school was an empty box—I don't know what is coincidence and what is not.

In England in 1978 it was important to keep up appearances. Go through the motions, with a solid though small coffin to lower as a focus for grief, if the actual bones were unavailable. I imagine. I imagine the deep brown grave, the empty brass-handled box. Perhaps the coffin was lacquered white, to denote the innocence of a child. I don't know because I wasn't there.

"Mum, did they recover the body?"

"Yes," she says. "We had Nicky's body."

If Mum said the word "Nicky" at irregular intervals, and she did, I never once heard my dad speak my brother's name. Not once. Whatever memories or mementos Dad kept were his alone, and his was the example we followed. Now, several years since he died, the rule of silence has lifted. I can rummage around, and I have the keys to the closets.

His study at one end of the bungalow remains largely untouched, and in an alcove behind a scroll-down door, formerly locked, there are three metal filing cabinets. Most of the drawers contain business correspondence or bank statements, but the bottom drawer of the corner cabinet has no obvious organizing principle. Letters from a Swindon rugby-club dispute with Ushers brewery (1980) are filed among Round Table itineraries from 1972. I pull out a green plastic bag.

Mum watches from the doorway. She has been sorting through Dad's papers and was the first to find the bag. "In the attic we have a red suitcase full of Nicky's stuff," Mum says. "And these papers your dad kept."

I separate out the contents: school reports, and a vinyl-covered ring-binder clamping a thick collection of commiseration letters. In among these is a Certified Copy of an Entry of Death. In the United Kingdom no document is more conclusive than a certificate signed by the Registrar, and the date of death is officially recorded as 18th August 1978. Nicky was alive, then he died, a fact now confirmed by two separate sources. There was a body:

Date and Place of Death: *18/8/78 Dead on Arrival Stratton Hospital, Bude*

Name and Surname: NICHOLAS PAUL BEARD

Date and Place of Birth: 23rd March 1969 SWINDON

Occupation and Home Address: Son of COLIN ANTHONY BEARD, BUILDER

Cause of death: **DROWNING in the Sea. Accident.**

I know the date and I've found the body.

I did not see him drown. The last time I saw Nicky he was alive, his head back, his neck tight, his lips clamped shut to keep out the water. Nevertheless, his body was recovered; he was removed from the sea, transferred to a vehicle and declared dead on arrival at the hospital in Bude. A signed document, registered in the sub-district of Stratton in the County of Cornwall, authenticates these facts. The form is filled in by hand, black ink, fountain pen, sometimes with block letters and sometimes not, with a note that an inquest was held on 4/10/78 and **Certificate received from G. H. St. L. Northey, Coroner for N-E Cornwall**.

The death certificate also gives me the date of my brother's birthday. 23rd March. I hold the page in my hand, not the certificate itself but a copy, signed by the Registrar (illegibly) "certified to be a true copy of an entry in a register in my custody," dated 20th November 1978. There is no arguing with this document, no reinterpretation. What I do feel is that our reaction to these facts can't have been entirely healthy, if I'm finding out the date of my brother's birthday from his death certificate.

Nevertheless this information, limited as it is, makes him more alive to me. I want more of him, whatever I can glean from this and other items of paperwork left behind. In the folder with the death certificate I find a typed letter from the Operations Manager of North Cornwall District Council, a reply to earlier correspondence from Mr. Beard, dated 7th October 1978, "concerning bathing conditions at Tregardock Beach."

Your observations will be presented to the Council's Beach Safety Working Party later this month.

I don't find a copy of the original letter, but I doubt Dad was commending the Council on their attention to health and safety. He wrote his letter of complaint, if that's what it was, six weeks after Nicky drowned, suggesting that by that time he'd already started looking for someone to blame. He wanted a story, with reasons and a villain, so perhaps he'd found a way to blame the Council. Their godforsaken beach was a death trap. Through negligence, the North Cornwall District Councilors had caused the death of his innocent child.

I want to see the beach for myself, so I borrow Mum's car again. "To visit the scene of the crime," I think. I'm behind the wheel of Mum's MX-5 heading south on the M5 asking myself why those are the words that occur to me: "the scene of the crime." It's just a phrase, because I have no evidence of criminal activity. **DROWNING in the Sea,** says the official verdict on the Entry of Death, the relevant section handwritten in black-ink copperplate: **Accident.**

I'm driving Mum's car to the scene of the accident. At times before now, on stressful occasions, I've fantasized about hiring a car and driving north. Any car will do, just point it north as far as north will go. The instinct may have been sound, only the direction was wrong. The deep southwest has the answers. I've used up the M5 and am running out of A30. On the A39 to Wadebridge, angular wind turbines on every rise remind me that 1978 is the past and these days we live in the future. I'm *beyond* the future—up close, the giant metal turbines are rusting.

The satnav tells me where to go, and when I crest a hill on the B3267 the horizon ahead is a slab of slate-gray Atlantic. In my head I hear my dad, and he says what he always says:

"Can you see the sea?"

"Yes, Dad, I can see the sea."

My destination is Port Isaac, a former fishing village on Cornwall's north coast. The holiday cottage where we stayed in 1978 was isolated, a gray house in a green valley with no other houses in sight, but I doubt we'd have stopped in the village more than twice in the course of a fortnight, once to look around, then again for souvenirs. When we needed provisions, Dad would show he was willing by leaving in the car and coming back with items from a list written by Mum, who'd tell him his strawberries and yogurts were overpriced. He had no idea about the realities of life, she'd say, to make a point and because she was right.

In Swindon, Dad would never go near the shopping, but on holiday he'd load the yogurts into the fridge and look hurt, as if no one understood his pain. The mood would pass. As a family we were together once a year, and it was important to stay calm, just as a month later he'd feel calm enough to write a letter of "observations" to the District Council about conditions on the beach that killed his son.

The Council's letter of response contained a valuable fact, which along with the death certificate made for a second important find in the green plastic bag. Mr. Pyman of the Camelford office names the real live beach where the drowning took place. Tregardock. Admittedly, my life had to be creaking and my dad had to die before I felt able to open the filing cabinet, but my day in Swindon with Mum had produced a decent opening result, enough to start piecing together the story we'd collectively conspired to forget.

Tregardock Beach, named in that letter, is north of Port Isaac, about halfway to Tintagel, which is nine or ten miles away. I check the name "Tregardock" as transcribed into my notebook, to remind myself where I'm going, then leave the notebook in the car as I wander through Port Isaac itself. The steep harbor streets don't bring back memories, and scratched across a metal One Way sign are the words *No English*, which is slightly hurtful, because the Cornish are welcome in Swindon any time.

The woman behind the counter in Nicky B's pasty shop tells me the village has changed, not always for the better. She blames TV tourism, because Port Isaac is the picturesque setting for a TV drama called *Doc Martin*—visitors get confused about what is real and what is not. "We get a different class of tourist now," she says. "They forget what they came for."

RICHARD BEARD

The fudge shop sells a map of the village as it appears in the TV series, where every façade is recognizable but different. The fudge shop is the pharmacy, and Doc Martin's surgery is the pottery. I'm not disappointed, though I've never seen the TV show and hadn't expected the village to be stuck in time, in the preservative of 1978.

The beach, however, is more of a worry. If the beach has changed, I'm frightened my possible encounter with the past will be lost. I'm equally frightened I'll find it exactly the same, opening up a direct route to memories deliberately erased.

I leave Port Isaac village without enriching a single fishing-themed tea-shop. The road north through Delabole runs parallel to the coastline, and as long as I try every left turn, I should be able to find my beach by trial and error. Sooner or later, without consulting a map, I'll find the beach about which the District Council, in 1978, received comments in writing from a recently bereaved father.

The first couple of lefts fail to reach the coast, ending at holiday cottages or farms. I five-point the Mazda between high thorn hedges, go back the way I came. I didn't bring a map because I felt the memory ought still to be within me, as a measure of the importance of the event, and of the dead. I'm looking for Tregardock, as named by the Council, but I'm not going to find it by car, not with the navigational skills of an eleven-year-old. I'd be more likely to recognize the route from the backseat of a Vauxhall Viva, no seat belt, towels on my lap and a beach ball under my feet. I end up at Trebarwith Strand, with its two surf shops and a pub. Should have brought a map. I decide to ask for directions.

Only I've forgotten the name of the beach, even though I recently looked it up in my notebook, which I left in the boot of the car, now parked in the car park. In the Trebarwith Port William Inn I find myself speechless. The beach I want starts with Tre- something, but so does most of Cornwall. I'm standing at the bar in the Port William Inn at Trebarwith Strand and the word—whatever it is—won't come out of my mouth. The name of the beach has vanished from my mind. Darkness is falling.

I don't find the beach that afternoon, and before daylight fades I need to pitch my tent. I drive back to Port Gaverne, and down the lane from the campsite I buy a pint at the Port Gaverne Hotel and order fish and chips, burger and chips—don't really care, as long as the plate is covered in chips, for the comfort. As my friend Dru once pointed out, all authentic English food is comfort food.

At a table in the corner I sip a pint of Doom Bar and make a start on the letters of condolence, which I've brought with me in their green plastic bag. There are so many, so much commiseration handwritten on various types of paper, from headed office stationery (*Hills Builders*) to lined double-punched A4 pads. I open notelets with floral designs (*all profits to Harlow Carr Gardens, Harrogate*) and ready-made cards from Hallmark (*At This Time of Sorrow*):

> *Although no words that we can say*
> *Will really ease your sorrow*
> *We know your faith will see you through*
> *To a happier tomorrow.*

I eat and I read. Occasionally I glance up at the mirror behind the bar and wonder what I look like. The most plausible resemblance is to a down-mouthed widower, escaping recent tragedy on a Cornish mini-break while rereading the sympathy of others one last time. This is the last time, then he'll put away the letters and move on.

I can't make the sadness stick. I find these letters from three decades ago too interesting. Some of the cards contain a discreet printed line from the Bible (*Thy rod and thy staff they comfort me*, Psalms 23:4), and because no trace of 1978 is beneath my attention, I note the stock code and penciled price on the back: B119, 20p. I hold up the heavier writing papers to the backlit bar, for the watermarks: Queen's Velvet, Three Candlesticks, Leach's Abingdon Parchment. The correspondence evokes a different era, just as many of the writers remain unmistakably themselves, whoever they may be.

I only heard about it this morning, Dorothy Clarke told me at the Coffee Morning.

Back then the death was gossip to some, and these letters are like gossip to me now: I'm tickled by the glimpse of characters from the past.

What an ending to your holiday, incidentally thank you for the card.

Not everyone had their best stationery to hand, but the urge to express written sympathy extends from work colleagues to people who live in the same Swindon street as us (they add the address, to be sure we can identify them as neighbors). Everyone is feeling terrible, from the PE teacher at school to the staff at Cross Street garage, which has the contract for the company vans. Bystanders on the beach (how did they get the Swindon address?) offer their *sincere condolences* and their *deep concern*, as do relations who in brackets add a reminder of who they are (*Aunt and Uncle*). Nicky's own friends communicate their sorrow as best they can: *Dear Mrs. Beard, I was very unhappy indeed and cried quite heartily.*

I can't remember what we were doing, or where we were when these letters flooded in. From the Bishop of Malmesbury, from the Swindon Town Club, the Committee and Members of the Clarendon Club, On Behalf of the Swindon Ladies' Circle, On Behalf of all members of the Inner Wheel Club, from the Swindon Conservative Association, the National Westminster Bank, my grandparents' neighbors who ran the market garden, teachers and their wives when we'd never have guessed they were married, from Lloyds Bank and various Anglican vicars and the Catholic priest of St. Savior's.

The old world, as of 1978, is filled with courtesy and legible handwriting, and the letters together summon a historical community of grief. *All of Swindon is grieving.*

A separate brown envelope contains a second impressive set of letters addressed to my grandparents. Gran has written on the outside of the envelope: "our letters, when you want to see them." Many are in handwriting identical to hers, signed Phyllis and Molly and Gladys, in true sympathy with my grandmother, Mabel.

My eyes are leaking, so I go to the bar for another pint, which seems to fix the problem. The reiteration of sorrow in these letters bombards me with the idea of grief, but fails to connect me for long to the actual feeling. I start comparing one letter with another, rating them for sincerity. I let my inner literary critic fend away the risk of genuine empathy.

The general consensus (*it has cast a gloom over Swindon*), with the notable exception of the Catholic priest, is that my parents and we the boys have suffered *a tragic loss, tragic circumstances, tragic news* and *a ghastly tragedy.* The loss, the circumstances, the news, the accident: a tragedy from every angle. At this sad time friends and acquaintances reach out with *most sincere condolences on the tragic death of your son.*

The death is tragic, the death. With that rare exception, "death" is the missing word. Loss, circumstances, news. The writers of the letters mean death.

Although we didn't know him.

I stop reaching for a sadness I don't feel and start looking for Nicky.

We all remember Nicholas at the Barbecue as a bright handsome boy with a lovely sense of humor.

Everything Nicky did he did well, be it sport, work, his music, or just kindness and good manners.

Nicky was extremely kind and helpful and a great conversationalist.

The safest response, I assume, is not to speak ill of the dead. Mum told me Nicky was behind with his schoolwork, and rubbish at sport. He dropped his catches. If he were the paragon these letters suggest, why dwell on his qualities and make the situation worse? Why would these people do that to me, years later in a quiet midweek pub?

The letters make Nicholas Beard shine, but I feel they're predictable, cheapening the experience of sudden death by saying what I'd expect them to say. The messages of condolence leave me cold, both the formulas (*no words could possibly console you*) and the exaggerations. *Nicky was, to me, the perfect schoolboy: bright, talented, and so enthusiastic, even when things were going badly.*

Death in these letters is character-forming, like a traditional English education, but no one knows how else to express the sense of loss. *Words seem so very inadequate.* I'll need to look elsewhere for the person Nicky truly was.

In Swindon, Mum had mentioned a red suitcase in the attic, but from my experience of teaching creative writing

I'm wary of shortcuts to Characterization. In particular, I distrust classroom exercises that involve a questionnaire:

- What does your character have in his pockets?
- What are your character's favorite clothes?
- How does your character feel about what he has in his pockets?
- How does your character feel about the way he looks?

This is how a fiction writer is taught to fully realize a nonexistent character, as part of the creative process. This step is essential, because if a character fails to come alive, no one will care when he dies.

My gran's funeral, up on the hill at Liddington, early 2002. Gran had been dying for months, and at the end she used to clutch my wrist with her waxy, misshapen fingers. "Why does the good Lord spare me?" She was ready to go, she said, and I believed her. So at the funeral sadness wasn't the only emotion I felt. After Gran's coffin was in the ground, outside in the graveyard, I saw Mum and my two brothers standing with heads bowed in front of Nicky's Celtic cross. I felt instant outrage, and no inclination to join them, though I knew my mum would have liked that. They were drawing attention to themselves, and to my dead brother, and this wasn't their day, or his. It was Gran's day. I kept to the tarmac path, and one of my cousins, whom I don't know well, said: "That's your brother, isn't it? I remember him, he was a good guy."

How could this cousin have formed an opinion? Nicholas was *nine*, and even those of us closest to him had barely known Nicky long enough to judge him as a person. For all my cousin knew, Nicky was a chump, or only intermittently a goodish kind of guy; any assessment of his character had to be provisional.

At Gran's funeral I didn't closely examine my anger, either with my immediate family or my cousin. I didn't question why it was preferable to move along, down the path to the Liddington Village Hall with the distant relatives and friends. I spurned Mum's impromptu family vigil, and missed another opportunity to study the wording on the gravestone. I told myself I wasn't interested, but in fact I wasn't ready. Now I feel I am.

Before setting out for Cornwall I'd reminded Mum of the red suitcase, the one she'd mentioned was in the attic, full of Nicky's stuff. The objects he'd left behind would help in getting to know him, at bridging all this distance — they were part of what had survived. I drove to Swindon and spent time looking for the hook to pull down the trapdoor to the attic. Found the hook, pulled down the trapdoor and then the ladder. I climbed into the loft space, and was transported back to the old family house.

When my parents moved — about 300 meters across Swindon as the crow flies — the attic moved with them. They resisted a clear-out at the time, and from one loft space to another the removal men shifted dismantled bedsteads, trunks and travel cots, boxes of cassette tapes, and many dented lampshades. Yes to all of those, here was the attic as it always had been, and yes to a cardboard box of Balinese shadow puppets, a *Cookbook for Boys* (1975), and Mum's scrapbooks of her wedding. Handmade clothes, it seems, are hard to throw away after the effort that goes into making them, and our enormous blue cloche for cheese may one day raise eyebrows on *Antiques Roadshow*. I find a newspaper cutting about a Swindon builder who went to work on his 100th birthday. I feel sorry for him, my own great-grandfather, and for the single-minded genes I may have inherited. Keep busy! Don't stop! One More Step Is Always Possible!

I fall briefly in love with a 1920s studio photograph of a beautiful, soft-faced woman called Madge. I don't know who she is. The attic is full of objects kept but not kept, that had value once when life was different and may again, if life ever changes.

No red suitcase.

"I'm sure it's there," Mum calls up. "Shiny, and square. It's red. You must have missed it."

"How big is it? What's inside it?"

"His letters, his schoolbooks. His blue cricket hat is in it."

"What blue cricket hat?" I poke my head through the trapdoor and look Mum in the eye upside down.

"You know. His blue cricket hat. The one he wore all the time."

I don't always recognize Mum's parallel version of the

past. I want documents, evidence, objects, but I climb down the ladder because there's no red suitcase.

Mum is apologetic. "We'd have to turn out the whole attic to be sure."

"Let's turn out the attic."

Mum is tired of the energy I'm devoting to the cause. I make another run through the attic, and in boxes and trunks find loose letters and a few photographs. Also, a blue school blazer (with his name tape in the back of the neck, *N. P. BEARD*, below a worn silk loop for hanging miniature blazers on low school pegs). The embroidered badge on the pocket says K, for Kingsbury Hill, his school before he moved to Pinewood. The pockets are empty.

Encouraged, I search behind the bedsteads, and between the folded handmade clothes. I don't find a carefully tended shrine of mementos, but nor has Nicky been systematically erased. He turns out to be in between, slipped to the bottom of cardboard boxes and in the linings of trunks, in the spaces behind old music systems and at the bottom of baskets of audio cassettes. He is forgotten, but not completely.

There is, however, no red suitcase. Nicky is fragmented, the scraps of his life scattered in pieces that until now no one has thought to gather together. We erased the accident at the beach, and along with the pain we effectively deleted Nicholas Paul Beard the person. We may not have meant to but we did, though not entirely.

In the attic I keep finding pieces of him. His birth certificate, and six Premium Bonds in his name, dated 3 June

1969. I'm amazed that before now no one has gone through these remnants looking for what's left of him, but no one ever has. The family has shared a desire to postpone, and possibly delay forever, the acknowledgment of Nicky's existence. And therefore also his nonexistence.

I'm old enough (at last) to appreciate more positive ways to cope with sudden death. Fear, I imagine, is one of the reasons we have distanced Nicky, but I did not shatter at the churchyard when I read the words on his gravestone, or when Mum revealed the date. We didn't need to be so frightened—the finds from the attic haven't overwhelmed me.

In fact, I feel rewarded by every object that connects to Nicky: he was real, he occupied a particular space of his own in the material world. Up in the attic I feel energized and useful. I pick out anything that might be relevant, and whenever I'm convinced I've salvaged all there is, I find something more. Certificates, schoolbooks, photographs I've never seen. In one of these photos I recognize his cricket bat, a polyarmored size-three Slazenger, and I go to the shed and there it is in the bucket of rotting sports equipment. The Slazenger has my younger brother Jem's initials painted on the back in red Airfix paint, but this is Nicky's bat. The rubber grip has perished, but I play a forward defensive and remember, from nowhere, that England's unshiftable opening batsman Geoffrey Boycott was Nicky's cricketing hero. Stubborn bastard, hard to dislodge.

Eventually, mired in dust and grime, back and knees aching, I have to accept I've covered every inch of the attic for surprise relics from Nicky's short life. At some point there are no further items to find, and my haul includes most of the objects Mum claimed for the elusive red suitcase. His blue cricket hat, for example, and his schoolbooks.

"We once had a recording of his voice," Mum says. "We knew it wouldn't last, the way you were then. We organized a quiz with the same format as *Mastermind*, and recorded everyone's turn to answer the questions. Recording took more preparation then than it does now, but we lost the cassette. Look, you found another hat."

The floppy camouflage hat is covered in cloth patches, badges of survival from family tours of duty: Corfe Castle, The Royal Tournament, the Talyllyn Railway.

"That's my hat," I say. "I just saw it, so I picked it up."

"That's Nicky's hat. I recognize the patches."

"It's mine."

We squabble for our conflicting narratives of the past, but the more evidence we unearth, I think, the less cause we'll have to squabble. The facts will speak for themselves. In the meantime our different memories betray the distance between us. "Did you chuck his other belongings out in one go, or gradually?"

"I don't know," Mum says. "I don't understand the question."

The attic pile of objects is not very big, despite Nicky's

nine years of life. In my own home I've had nine-year-old boys and could hardly move in their bedrooms for the stuff they have.

"You didn't have a solemn ritual sometime after he died? Maybe an afternoon you put aside to dismantle his bedroom, to decide what was worth keeping?"

An absence surrounds the odds and ends I've collected together. Nicky's casual clothes are missing, as is his toothbrush, his football boots, his light reading and comics. Where are his biodegradables, and his disposable everyday life?

"Did you have a tight-lipped clear-out, dumping his comb and pencil case without even looking? Maybe you got someone in, to do it as a favor, or you paid someone. Take the emotion out of it."

I stop before I upset Mum more than I already have. I can hear myself making up stories on her behalf, and that's not the idea. Stick to the facts, now that I know from the graveyard and the death certificate that facts in themselves will not destroy us. The emotion they've so far failed to evoke feels like an outlet silted up and blocked through deliberate neglect. I look again at my Nicky pile, and I'm not disappointed, considering I climbed into the attic with few expectations beyond a single red suitcase. No suitcase, so this pile is all we have, and no more. On reflection, the pile amounts to almost nothing. I feel I'm reaching out for Nicky, but there's never enough of him there.

I concentrate on what I have, the boy in pieces.

Three baby shoes, a pair in white and one solitary blue shoe.

A blue tracksuit top (with a *J. I. BEARD* name tape, but I'm sure I remember this as the top Nicky wore in Cornwall)—it has a distinctive hexagonal patch saying *GO*, in green, sewn onto the left breast.

An invitation card with *Nicholas* written in italic red to my great-grandfather's 100th birthday celebration. The date of my great-grandfather's birth is misprinted and overwritten in blue biro (presumably on every invitation): 18 April 1878. As a family, it looks like we're weak on dates.

A framed certificate from Devizes Junior Eisteddfod 1976, *Piano Solo, Under 9, 80 — Merit.*

School bills.

A small transparent plastic bag: *Cash's 72 Name Tapes. By Appointment to Her Majesty the Queen Manufacturers of Woven Name Tapes.* In blue— *N. P. BEARD.* Unopened.

The Empire "Cumulative" Cricket Scoring Book, for invented cricket matches. Nicky has filled in dates for the new season—1978–79—but of the book's possible 100 innings, only two games have started.

A selection of letters to and from.

Photographs, many single photographs, mostly dog-eared or creased. Others in a cardboard scrapbook, the prints glued or Sellotaped at the corners, the Sellotape as brown as the glue.

A pocket-sized Letts Schoolboys' Diary 1978, bound in red plastic.

The blue floppy sun hat Mum called his cricket hat, but I'm not sure it is. It fits on my head. The label inside says Harrods, so the hat was school uniform, bought on our yearly trip to London. We didn't go to London, as such. We drove up the M4 and parked at the Knightsbridge NCP, walked round to Harrods, bought school uniforms, and ate a roast-beef lunch in the Georgian carvery. Harrods was London, just as Cornwall was holiday England.

Two newspaper cuttings: **Surf Boy is Fourth Victim** is one headline. The other is **Holiday Boy, 9, swept to death.**

A blue-peaked gray school cap, name-taped, from *Gorringes of Victoria, School and College Outfitters, Phone Vic. 6666, London, SW*1, which looks antique even to me, and I'd have worn something similar. Size 6¾, with oil from Nicky's hair shiny in the rust-black lining.

A folder marked **Nicholas Beard, Termly Reports.** Another reason not to die young: what will survive of us is our school reports.

The morning after failing to find Tregardock Beach by car, I leave the Mazda at Port Gaverne and decide to walk. The South West Coast Path follows the cliffs north across National Trust land, and I'm persuaded by the idea of approaching the beach on foot. I won't have to talk to anyone. Also, if I take every track that turns left between here and Tintagel, I can't help but find my beach. Though it won't be straightaway—I estimate I have three or four miles of tough up-and-down hiking, the grass knee-high with bluebells and red campion, and on the higher sections complicated with brambles, a plant with a liking for Britain's climate.

In the absence of a map I'm relying on memory, and from up on the coastal path I have a panoramic view of every cove and inlet. The blue-white sea smashes into Cornish rock. I may have misremembered the broad sand beach, elaborating a haven where the rest of the family was out of danger, but I decide I can't afford not to trust my memory. If I'm wrong about what I remember, what else might I always be wrong about?

Originally, I'd assumed the sea and the beach were within walking distance of the rented holiday house, but in the attic I'd found a map hand-drawn by Dad. He'd written out clear directions from Swindon to The Mill, denoting the house with a rectangle to the south side of Port Isaac. Tregardock, on 18th August 1978, must have been a special outing by car to a beach worth the journey. I'm therefore not expecting to see the house, not today.

From high on the path I dismiss one cove after another; I feel physically sick. I'm anxious I'll never find the place that I settled in my memory. Or that I will. Reality feels like an enemy, a toxin identifiable at a distance, like a bad smell. My body prepares to reject the past, and I experience a sense of physical blockage in my heart, in my throat. As I walk along I clutch my chest and cough. Rain starts to fall.

Danger
Cliff Liable to Subsidence

The fence is on the wrong side of the coastal path, protecting the sheep in the fields, which means no protection for walkers between the path itself and a drop to the fizzing ocean below, one misjudged step away. One more step is always possible. I could throw myself into the sea and drown. I could get blown off the cliff and drown. I'm assaulted by fear, by which I mean imagined stories that end badly, in particular for me.

I haven't planned ahead, I don't have a decent map, but it helps that no one gets lost on a coastal path. Now I'm here, I do sincerely want to find Tregardock Beach, and the smaller cove beyond it. I want to stop guessing, or imagining, but if I found that easy I'd have made careful preparations and brought an Ordnance Survey map. I'd have gone directly to the place I want to reach.

Over every new headland my heart lurches, but with each fresh vista of inlets I don't see sand and I'm thinking: the beach can't be that big, because these coves are tiny. The rain eases but the wind is up, skimming foam off the waves before they shatter into cliffs. The path dips and a track to the left feels familiar. I walk along it, heart thudding. No beach at the end, a false trail.

Wherever this beach is, we had a decent walk to get there. Every disappointing inlet means the next is more likely to be the one true place. I start shouting "Fuck!

Fuck!" as if from sudden-onset Tourette's. Maybe my dad wrote his letter of observations about the wrong beach. Of course this is possible, because at the moment of the drowning he wasn't there. He doesn't feature in any memory of what I know. Fuck! Fuck!

I did not imagine I would react like this.

By now I'm walking so slowly I laugh at myself, which turns to coughing and doubling up and I think I'm going to choke. I can barely haul myself over the stiles. I'm terrified of moving forward, closer to the past. Such a muddle, such chaos. I want to keep the grief at a distance, if grief it is, so I sit down out of the wind to write some notes, and the written word gives me an excuse for not walking further. Then I put my writing away and I do trudge further, but dragging my heavy heart onward, as far as a weathered 2 × 4 pounded stoutly into the coastal turf. **TREGARDOCK, 1 MILE.** The letters are burned into the wood vertically. There can be no doubt.

The beach is beyond the next promontory. I hope so much to find it disappointing, and that coming back will be no big deal. It's no big deal at all, really. Everything's all right, as we've been convincing ourselves for years. Don't feel bad, just as Mum told me when I didn't need to be told. That's how I've chosen to remember my initial response. On the night Nicky drowned I was sleeping like a baby, then I woke up. I wasn't scared. I wasn't upset, or a mess of loss and grief and despair. Not me. I wanted the toilet. Mum, honestly I'm fine.

Tregardock Beach will be a massive disappointment. I will feel nothing, again, and I can cope with that because disappointment is within my emotional range. I have the experience.

School reports offer half-truths at best, but I'm grateful for any source that can tell me more about Nicholas Beard. The reports take in two schools from Spring '74 through Summer '78, and I read these assessments of Nicky's character in chronological order, hoping to see a person developing from the child. The early days are of limited interest, not much to see except a cosset of headmaster's platitudes — *he settled into school life quickly and easily, a promising pupil.*

Then, within a year of starting school, Mum's "difficult child," doomed to a life of banking or homicide, is a *delightful and able boy*, and from 1975 the reports have a category, almost too good to be true, marked **Emotional Development.** He is *Well Controlled. No problems,* and the next term *No problems at all.* He is a sound, controlled child, so not, at this age, the character type to run alone and reckless into a dangerous and raging sea. The future, with hindsight, can lure headmasters into unwitting moments of pathos — *he continues to do well, and his future looks bright,* a comment that in the drought summer of 1976 is surpassed by Nicky's form teacher: *He has made a courageous effort to swim and can manage half a width (under water!).*

Funny, Mrs. Huxley. Bet you regret that now.

In 1977 Nicky starts boarding at Pinewood School, aged eight and a bit, and in Form 1 is *a little overconfident*. The decisive Final Order, however, at the end of the year, sees him rise to second in a class of ten. He is *a natural cricketer* (a bowler), *above average*.

Mum has it all wrong, mourning a boy who never was. A banker? He was *a caring and very helpful young pupil*. A murderer? He was a *lively, cheerful boy*.

We forget. Nicholas is a brainbox with a talent for sport. Anyone at school with him, like me, could on reflection have told Mum that this was so, only we never took time to reflect. I'm glad that the school reports bear witness, because Nicky is otherwise ghostly in his absence.

I have sensed him (when I allowed myself to do so, until now at the edge of my vision) as weak, vulnerable, his defining quality being an inability to save himself from drowning. He hasn't done anything to alter this impression, not since 1978. From the age of nine he became meek and unassuming. Of course he did. In nearly four decades he hasn't opened his mouth, hasn't thrown his weight around. Inevitably, unable to impose any fresher identity, he can become a nondescript cipher in a corner.

The school reports from 1978 tell a different story: he wasn't like that at the time. Despite the coded evasions of the form — *After a rather erratic start...* — what builds is a picture of a boy who was overconfident, competitive, but also properly homesick. The teachers try to help him settle.

They give him a new name to make him feel he belongs. On his tombstone he is Nicholas Paul Beard, and he is Nicky in my memory. At boarding school he becomes Beard minimus, defined by Latin as much as by his family. After Beard major and Beard minor (me), Nicky is the latest and least of the Beard brothers.

No wonder he'd want to make his presence felt. His first term's report is accompanied by a letter from the headmaster, in which the school secretary's heavy hand has bashed indents in the paper with the hard-type keys:

20th May 1977

Dear Mr. and Mrs. Beard,

I do like the latest Beard model, Mark III. But, this one is a little too self assured I believe and hope that time will wear him down just a little in this respect before he emerges as charmingly frank and straightforward as Mark I. I have been encouraged by the way he has settled down here. He has seemingly taken all well in his stride. We look forward to some very happy days with him here.

Yours sincerely,

Geoff Walters

Nicky's schooling unfolds as a contest between the self-assurance and the wearing down. In the reports *settled down* reads like a boarding-school euphemism, meaning the tipping point at which Nicky stops weeping for his mummy and daddy, who for his own benefit have lured him away from the home comforts of his bedroom to abandon him in an unheated mock-Tudor mansion. He'll soon overcome his sadness. And that, from the school's point of view, is greatly to be encouraged.

Spring Term 1978, with fewer than six months to live: *He works well and settles once the "goodbyes" are well over and done with.* The hint is there again, the nudge: Nicky does not settle immediately, as one would hope. He does eventually forget the wrench of saying goodbye, but how long that will take is anybody's guess. Days, probably, for the farewells to genuinely fade, but possibly weeks.

The teachers are less evasive when they later come to write their letters of condolence. The boy is dead, so no harm in admitting that he once openly showed emotion. *I remember how touching it was to see him biting his lip and fighting back tears at the beginning of term at school and then bravely facing facts.*

And in 1978 the facts to be faced were that your parents have left the premises without you. The facts at Pinewood School were that none of these boarders would be going home for at least a month, and then only for Sunday lunch and back in time for chapel (for the second time that day). The way to handle emotion was to fight back the tears.

Please, Nicky, be brave and don't make a scene. I once saw a small boy screaming while horizontal, both hands clamped to the door-handle of a Volvo while his father tried to pull him off by the legs. That boy didn't look very settled, not as the new term began. He had fallen short of the required standard: biting his lip and bravely facing facts.

Now that the school reports bring this to mind, I do remember Nicky being homesick. He could be sniveling and weak. I despised his weakness, because I was weak and miserable too. Unlike him, however, I knew how to hide it. The surest way was to mock the youngest boarders, those in with Nicky and he in with them. Crybabies blubbing for Mummy; look at Beard min—he's a blubber. Nicky hadn't the first idea about suppressing emotion. He was an embarrassment, and two years was a dangerous-sized gap between us. I was old enough to feel superior, big enough not to fear retaliation.

As a summary of his character at that age, Nicky was excellent at sport and lessons, but he missed his mummy. I missed my mummy, but I wasn't going to show it. According to the school magazine—and I'd borrowed 1975–1980 from the obliging music teacher, Mr. Field—my childhood was full of busy displacement activities, not just competitive running and jumping but also the drawing of a pen-and-ink knight in a stained-glass window, an artwork of which I was inordinately proud. The school kept body and mind fully occupied: in 1978 the magazine had a crossword in Latin.

Not recorded in the magazine for public consumption was the way we taunted a classmate of Nicky's for smelling of urine; another (a day boy) we mocked without mercy for his anti-allergy lunchbox containing Mummy's special sandwiches. We loathed the taint of home on anyone new, the reminder that somewhere close they had loving parents who respected their childish needs.

Nicky is soon compensating in the same way I did, by proving how strong he is. By Spring 1978 he's first in his term's Final Order, and first in every subject except Maths (fourth). First in French, History, Geography, Scripture — all first. First in English, and that's my subject, where *he is never satisfied unless he is top!* He has a *somewhat arrogant manner*, but why shouldn't he, because he's *active and well coordinated, and always gives* 100% *effort.*

I end up trusting what his teachers say because this level of scrutiny is rare. Nine adult professionals think carefully about my living, breathing brother and three times a year they deliver a judgment in writing. No change goes unobserved. He's a terrible loser, is Nicholas Beard, Beard minimus. From this distance I admire his *competitive spirit* and his will to win: *he must learn to curb his temper when things do not go his way.* But I doubt I admired him at the time.

He must learn to accept defeat more graciously when he meets it. He holds his own and *does well to compete with others who are often physically much larger than he is.* Like an older brother, for example. I start to hesitate about taking on my younger crybaby brother, because with his relentless 100 percent effort and his coordination and competitive spirit, he's in with a chance of winning.

Stubborn little bastard, yes, I remember that now. Wiry, indefatigable, he keeps on coming. And, Christ, the tears and tantrums when the natural order prevails and I'm top dog. Hard cheese, suck it up. I'm older and bigger than you. I'm alive.

A mile on from the wooden post announcing Tregardock Beach is a second Tregardock marker pointing left along a narrow track. Yesterday, in the car, I couldn't find the word, let alone the place. Today the National Trust is leaving nothing to chance. Tregardock Beach is aggressively signposted. Turn left here.

I turn right and walk uphill, away from the booming ocean, and within twenty minutes I reach a farmhouse at the end of a narrow lane. I wonder about parking, for a lumbering Vauxhall Viva or a '77 Jaguar, an S-plate special. Tight into the hedge, I reckon, as close as the paintwork allows, keeping the lane free for farm vehicles. Four boys tumble out of the lane-side door. The boot is stuffed with bags of rolled-up towels, a wicker basket with the picnic in tin foil and Tupperware, buckets and spades, cricket bat.

Leave the beach ball, more trouble than it's worth. Everyone ready? Then away we go.

But first, these many years later, a deep breath. From here where the cars park it's a fair old trek to the sea, and I identify a possible cause for drowning right there. A nine-year-old boy with skinny legs exhausted from the walking, the running, the cricket, and therefore lacking power in his swimming kick. The Beard family's grand outing to

Tregardock Beach, at the pace of the slowest walker (Jem, 6), began with a twenty-minute hike. Twenty-five, if we keep testing the grass seeds and refuse to do as we're told.

Before I set out for the beach, I try to flatten the emotion by telling myself this isn't the first time since 18th August 1978 that I've been in this place, about to follow this path. Today is not an extraordinary day, and I have nothing to fear. That's what I tell myself, then I wait for the payback from years of emotional repression. The dividend for shutting down emotions as a routine response is invincibility at moments of stress. This is a psychological gamble, in England embraced as a gift. The English don't fall apart, our most prized national characteristic. Look at history and see how economically productive this quality can be.

Except now *is* the first time I've stood at the top of this path since 1978. I can't predict what will happen when reality collides with memory. For now, on this sunny Cornish morning, I've put aside the paper evidence to search out and try to inhabit an elusive first person, the me who long ago was here.

The track starts at a kissing gate, with rusted hinges as old as I am. Then leads downhill along the side of a field, the wild grasses ripe and tempting. I strip the seeds neatly into my fingers, and liberate them into the field on the breeze.

A stream gurgles to the left of the track, and then the track itself becomes slate bedrock through a head-high tunnel of gorse. I cross the coastal path, where I first turned right and away from the sea, I keep moving toward a gully cutting a V in the cliffs. As I reach the indent a view of the Atlantic opens, and below me the crumbling track traverses a steep incline, angling toward water breaking on the slick black sealskin of rocks.

I start crying. Just like that, no warning. Keep walking, keep moving. I don't know what the sudden tears mean, but they're strangely welcome. Why else did I come here? I take a step and another step down the slope and now I'm blubbing my heart and eyes out, but my legs keep moving, then I call out loud for my mum. Out loud into the air over the edge of the island landmass, over the heaving sea, and this spasm of harsh salt tears lasts roughly fifteen seconds. I don't have the strength, I imagine, to let go for any longer. I cut out my weeping and wipe my eyes and tell myself to shut the fuck up. This is no way to deal with emotional stress, or not a way I recognize. I wipe my eyes and pull myself together, because this is the place.

The end of the track is marked by an orange-and-white life buoy stuck on a wooden post. *Public Rescue Equipment In case of Emergency call 999 and ask for the Coastguard.* Maybe my dad's letter had some effect, especially if the previous sign said *Run Up to the Farm and Knock on the Door.* I check my phone: no signal. So in case of emergency I may be running to the farm. *Please take your rubbish home with you.*

To the right of the life buoy are steps carved into solid rock, with the route to the beach indicated by a small yellow arrow. On this particular day, at this time, the steps descend into a surge of ocean. Not a single inch of sand is visible, only white water on rock.

This is definitely the place, but the tide is in. I hadn't considered tides. I'm an inland visitor ignorant of the sea, and of the daily rhythms that expose then submerge my long-lost Tregardock, revealing the beach then hiding it from view again. I ought to stand by the life buoy and wait for this analogy to germinate, for the afternoon tide to roll back and exhibit the secret expanse of beach, disclosing my past, laying bare my memories. The natural world offers up these correlations effortlessly—the outside is the inside, because everything connects. What is now submerged will soon become apparent.

Gradually, even as I wait and watch, a thin stretch of wet brown sand shows itself, but I've seen enough for today. The beach looks like it may emerge as huge, just as I remember, especially if the water recedes beyond the brackets of each individual cove. A vast strand may appear here, proof that my memory is accurate, but the tide has only recently turned and it's far too early to say for sure.

Besides, I have a meeting arranged at The Mill. After the passing of so much time, I'd rather not be late.

From his schoolbooks I know what Nicky had in his mind when he died. Seven is three less than ten; Old King Cole was a merry old soul; the wild duck or mallard lives mostly on water, and the female is not so bright.

Name *Beard min*, Subject *Words and Sentences*, Form *Transition A*.

He knows the position of the polestar, and can spell *pence* and *France* and *police*. He can tell the time, as tested and ticked in his earliest English workbook — *it is 4 o'clock and at 4 o'clock I have my tea*. He has sufficient motor skills to cut out his footprint in colored card and measure its area at 118 square centimeters. His foot in April 1978 is about the height of a standard paperback book. He can follow instructions like *draw a line 10 cm long*, and has spent time on conundrums that are harder than at first they look: how many 2s in 12?

His schoolbooks, manufactured by Philip and Tacey Ltd, England, are bound in washed-out green or red card, and by the age of nine Nicky's head is buzzing. His brain finds room for the history of Edward III, Possessive Adjectives in French, St. Aidan. He can tell right ($5 \times 5 = 25$) from wrong ($650 - 431 = 121$).

Nicky leaves traces of his existence in diagrams, drawings, numbers, words. Look at him, making his mark, in pencil or washable ink, but what can be learned from schoolbooks? *Answer the question with a complete sentence:* the books may reveal the boy who Beard min was.

Only Nicky was just doing what his teachers had told him to do. As I flip through the books, learning little I didn't already know, I start to feel that every hour Nicky spent in a classroom was wasted. At some point, all children at school feel this, usually while staring out of a window at a tree, and every child is right at the time. Life can end abruptly, without warning, at any given moment. Instead of rote-learning *Farming in the British Isles,* Nicky would have existed more richly outside, throwing his penknife into the bark of a giant redwood. I don't know if he owned a penknife. I didn't find one in the attic.

Subject *English Composition.* I have a prejudice in favor of the truths offered by fiction. I expect creative writing to offer insights into character and worldview, so I put aside *Maths* and *Geography* to pay closer attention to *English* and *Word Building* and *All My Own Stories.* These books have been locked away for decades, where no one has thought to read them. Like unearthed sacred texts, I discover, they never quite deliver on their promise of revelation.

Much of Nicky's writing is handwriting practice, about Lucy Locket who lost her pocket but Kitty Fisher found it. *Nothing in it, nothing in it, Just the ribbon round it.* Otherwise, his stories have a simplicity that suggests he struggles with the slipperiness of fiction: *One day a cat and a dog went for a walk down the road they met a man the man said where are you going the cat said down the road.*

Nicky is more naturally a chronicler, a nonfiction specialist:

Yesterday we went to Lydiard Park and we played rugby and Timmy and Peter won. Then Timmy said I would like to go home so we went home.

For Nicky, these true-life adventures are recent, and always will be. I trust him to document domestic life in Swindon in the 1970s as if it were yesterday:

Yesterday we went to Gran because Mummy went to Little Cote then we came home with Jeremy then we had some sandwiches and we watched TV.

We had some sandwiches and we watched TV. That's the way we lived, and Nicky feels no urgent pressure to elaborate.

In the absence of revealing fictions, I hope for doodles — free-range thoughts trapped like fossils in the strata of yellowing pages. I look for Nicky's inner life betrayed by unguarded moments, and eventually I'm rewarded. At the back of an early English schoolbook from when he was about seven, I find five loose sheets of Basildon Bond. Nicky has been daydreaming. Yes, I think, here at last, his authentic character exposed. He has decided, for no obvious reason, to judge his family, though in pencil, as if not entirely confident of his verdicts. This is new: he's experimenting out of school on loose sheets of letter-writing paper.

Each member of the family has a separate page, though

"Mummy" and "Daddy" are blank. Perhaps the task of providing an honest description of his parents was too daunting for a seven-year-old (or a son of any age, for that matter). As for brothers, Nicky decided his observations were worth putting on record. We each have our separate page:

Timothy
Fat well you can't say that.
Very untidy but allright
Supose he's all right.

I've studied Nicky's end-of-term reports, and now in his schoolbooks he reports right back, making a note on each of his brothers. It's only fair he should have his say. Jem is five and still at home, but Nicky has an opinion:

Jeremy
Adventurous he'll be allright
When he grows up
He likes to get ahead with everything.

Nicholas Beard — Beard minimus — knows his own mind:

Richard
Tough and stupid
Sporting but silly
Very much like Timothy

Thanks, Nicky, you're entitled to your opinion, which I won't dismiss simply because you're dead. Stupid?

Tough and stupid. Emotionally, yes, fair comment and true and increasingly evident. *Sporting but silly*, and my silliness will allow sport to distract me for years to come, without end in fact. *Very much like Timothy.* I was never fat, so I must be *allright, suppose he's all right.*

Though Nicky never actually goes so far as to write that down, not on the page he dedicates to me.

The holiday home we rented in the summer of 1978 features in contemporary newspaper reports of the drowning—*His parents, staying at The Mill, Port Isaac, were on the beach nearby when tragedy struck on a sunny afternoon* (*Western Evening Herald*, 19th August 1978). From the Swindon attic, I also had the page of directions handwritten by Dad.

I'd checked on Google, but the Cornwall Tourist Board had no Port Isaac holiday house registered as The Mill. Instead the Internet gave me The Mill, Port Isaac, as a "small working farm." The owners had a barn conversion to let, and inquiries were welcome. I'd therefore picked up the phone and inquired about the barn; I explained about the dead brother. The owners said drop in, come and see us any time.

So I did.

My dad's directions—*The Mill, Port Isaac, ROUTE*—were on a piece of foolscap accounting paper folded in four. I smoothed out the creases, and the Cornish sunshine picked out splinters of copper in the black ink of the handwriting.

Dad was very exact, each instruction a separate pre-computer bullet point: —**Recommend,**—**Follow,**—**A30,**—**Approx 3 miles…,** and on this occasion he'd made an effort to render his dreadful handwriting legible, mostly by putting important words in capitals: *RIGHT, STRAIGHT ON, ST. ENDELLION, DO NOT.* The middle of the page is a drawing of the roads between the A39 and the coast, with the final destination marked like treasure, at the end of a dotted line with an X in a box: *MILL!*

This exclamation mark is out of character. The map must be intended for Mum, though I don't know why they'd be traveling apart. For now, on the page, Dad is making an upbeat effort at a jaunty holiday spirit: *"RIGHT to narrow lane and gate to field is STRAIGHT ON as shown. LEFT in field along hedge and through gate down gully—MILL AHOY!!"*

The final flourish from a Swindon builder with no sea-faring experience is cheerily nautical. Though to be fair, in 1978 he couldn't have foreseen that the education he was buying for his children would later allow his second son to pick apart his language and punctuation, as used on a casual map. I was only eleven. My likeliest future still involved pricing labor and materials for kitchen conversions.

Could have, should have, but I can't change the past. Following my Dad's map, looking for The Mill, I go wrong. There's no good reason to miss the turning because

Dad has written an impeccable set of directions, but I end up in Port Quin, not where I want to be. I reread the final section, this time more carefully. *Turn sharp RIGHT before Church.* Trust your Dad to know where you're going.

Like the map says, the *narrow lane and gate to field is STRAIGHT ON as shown.* I turn *LEFT* in the field along the hedge, over a cattle-grid and onto concrete strips for the tires. On the steep track down into the valley the spontaneous tears make a comeback. Cry and drive, and I'm sobbing for the unbidden idea of an eleven-year-old boy in a police car bumping over these ruts, heart overflowing with grief. Any eleven-year-old, not just me, so I'm not sure if this is an idea or a memory. I may be about to find out, depending on what happens *through gate down gully—MILL AHOY!!*

The tears stop as abruptly as they started. I wipe my eyes. In memory, The Mill is a gray house in a green valley with no other buildings in sight. Mum had remembered a cottage covered in clematis, but at the end of the lane I park outside a rectangular white-painted farmhouse with green shutters and guttering. Up to the left the house is raised on a narrow shelf of land, and the lane runs on, narrowing to a pedestrian track that descends past the sewage works to Port Isaac.

Bertie and Jim Watson, who bought the house at the end of 1978, greet me at the garden gate. My repressed self follows them politely through the gate, onto a flagstoned path, onward past geraniums and a plastic rain barrel to the open kitchen door. As we did all those years ago, they use the kitchen door at the back as their main entrance. I remember this part of the house as gray stone, and when I recognize it I feel a flood of relief. Right house, definitely.

"We like old houses," Bertie says, a little defensively, "and think they should stay that way."

I see the building isn't in great repair, and I'm glad: traces of 1978 should be easier to identify.

Bertie is originally from Hertfordshire, and her husband Jim from Cheshire. She's eighty now, though looks twenty years younger, and hints at a bustling former life. Before she and Jim moved to Cornwall to keep pigs and ewes, she tells me, she used to be an estate agent.

What strikes me about the house, before we go in, is the absence of flat space for ball games. I can envisage a few minutes of French cricket, perhaps, on a patch of grass where the washing line is. But I hate French cricket and always have, mainly because it isn't cricket. The game is limited to skills so basic my gran could join in and, without runs to be scored, no one is rewarded for actually playing well. In that sense French cricket is unfair, because talent is leveled out. After a few days of not cricket, we'd have wanted to play a real game, in earnest, winner takes all. Nicky isn't the only competitive spirit in the family.

Inside the house, nothing is immediately familiar. Bertie and Jim have tried to help by going easy on the redecoration, and I take it slowly, head cautiously round the kitchen door for what could be an emotional ambush. The flagstones are original to at least 1978, and probably a hundred years earlier. The blue Belfast sink has sat beneath the window for generations.

Through the kitchen, an interior doorway leads into an open-plan space on either side of a staircase, again with the original floors and beams. No carpets. The hard edges of stone and wood were not projections of my hardened mind. So far, so good. My memory has some of the facts right, which is reassuring, but also I suspect grief to be indestructible and endlessly patient. Should I blunder into ghosts, however intentionally, I worry about the emotional impact. But wherever the feelings went, it seems I didn't leave them lying about at The Mill in Port Isaac.

"Yes," I say. "That's very kind. I'd love a cup of tea."

Bertie makes the tea and I apologize for my state of distraction. The last time I set foot in this house was not a happy time, and I hope she understands. Having said that, the long years of family denial mean I don't know how much of the original experience is left inside me. I've come here as terrified of finding nothing as I am of finding something, and don't want to discover that my dead brother has no enduring emotional reality. That isn't the information I want to retrieve.

"Maybe we should have tried counseling," I say, worried I've been impolite, paying more attention to the house than to Bertie.

"I'm not sure counseling is a good idea," Bertie says, as

if she'd made up her mind years ago. "Everyone has their own way of dealing with grief."

We sit outside on the porch with a view of the green hill opposite, and Bertie tells me a story about the nature of chance. She thinks she's telling me about buying the house, and on the surface she is: she's a reliable narrator about property because of her former profession. She and Jim made their first offer for The Mill in May 1978, three months before the Beard family arrived in Cornwall on holiday. This information fits with a letter I found in Dad's filing cabinet. It was sent by the former owner of The Mill, Mr. A. D. Gill of Petersfield, Hampshire, on 10th October 1977. Mr. Gill makes a note of Dad's interest in the house for August 1978, *but as yet have made no firm plans for next summer.* He suggests my dad get in touch *next May or thereabouts,* so as late as May 1978 Mr. Gill couldn't commit to letting the house for August.

He was hoping to sell it, and if he had, The Mill would not have been available for holidaymakers in the summer of 1978. My dad wouldn't have made the late booking. None of the events that August would have happened as they did. Fate would have intervened.

Jim and Bertie's sale fell through, the house remained a holiday let, down came the inland grockles and their little boy drowned. I hear Bertie's house-buying history as a story of luck gone bad. Fate was against us, but only by a couple of months.

That autumn Jim and Bertie tried a second bid, and the

sale went through by the end of the year. Mr. Gill, possibly discomforted by the summer's events, may have accepted a lower price. But I have no evidence. All I know is that Jim and Bertie came in too low with their original offer to save Nicky's life. If Mr. Gill had sold them The Mill in May 1978, as they'd hoped, the Watsons would still be here now, but I would not. Chance, bad luck, I don't know what to call it, but those are the words that apply. Nothing has to be.

"Of course you can look around," Bertie says. "Take your time, I'll leave you to it."

About two-thirds of the way up to the second floor, the stairs split in opposite directions. The branch to the left leads to my bedroom. I know this. Adults to the right, children to the left. I'd have crossed this staircase (down to the split, then up again) to get to the bathroom—the bathroom is next to Mum and Dad's bedroom, via the right-hand staircase. When I see the layout of the stairs and the bathroom, I realize how easy it was for Mum to intercept me, and how plausible for me to seed the idea that nothing was wrong. I wasn't looking for my mummy; this was the route to the bathroom. Mum misunderstood the situation. I needed a pee, that's all. Just along there, in the bathroom right beside her bedroom.

Though obviously that wasn't all, or I wouldn't be in The Mill nearly forty years later with Bertie and Jim. Children are not tougher than they look.

I'm confident there's valuable material here for me, at the very least a real-life setting to fit around that midnight memory. Back downstairs, in the dining-room section of the open-plan ground floor, I stand in a shaft of sunlight from the window. My eyes flit from the table to the chairs, to the kitchen door, to the table, to the chairs, from the present to the past, peeling back the years.

Bertie pops her head round the door. "Everything all right?"

"Was this always the dining room?"

"There used to be an oval table when we first arrived."

"Could I sit down for a minute?"

"Of course you can," Bertie says. "More tea?"

Oval, round. My past exists. I own a former self, once trapped in this very room, at a holy communion with an ordained vicar. I remember now. I think of the ceremony as a kind of séance.

Then I see it.

The chair I'm sitting on looks toward the staircase and the kitchen beyond, and a flush rises in my face. My heart skitters. An adult stranger, a dressed-down minister of God, has the light of the kitchen doorway behind his head. It is actually difficult to make out his face. My dad is standing beside him, near the stairs, making a speech. I remember this. He said that unbeknown even to Mum, he'd always written a diary. Now he wanted to record our thoughts about Nicky. One at a time, we should think of a memory or observation, presumably while Nicky remained fresh in our minds. This must have been the day after, not much later.

My eleven-year-old self is squeezed between bodies on both sides, but the question progresses around the oval table. Here it comes, closer and closer whether I like it or not, and I can't escape. What did Nicky mean to me? That's Dad's prompt. Think of a memory that's worth writing down.

My turn. In the silence everyone looks, waiting for my contribution. I don't know. I'm not ready for this. I don't know what Nicky meant to me, or what I'm supposed to say.

I punched him in the face. Share this.

Earlier that year Nicky had stood in the doorway of my Swindon bedroom, and from inside my territory, with a closed fist, I punched him straight in the face. I had no reason to do so. My bedroom was at the end of the corridor, beside the toilet, and he came down to tell me something. It was time to go out, probably, and we were wanted downstairs. Whatever the message was, I stood and looked at him. I punched him hard, like on television. Boom.

He did not fall down, and I was instantly terrified. Nicky bawled and ran toward the stairs, while I hid inside my wardrobe, pulling the door closed behind me. I crouched in the darkness behind the coats and jeans, because Mum would be up to punish me. There would be no end to the justice coming my way, so I hunched in the dark narrow closet, invisible, miserable. My mum shouted my name. She was coming, I knew it, she was coming to pay me back.

Except she wasn't. I don't doubt she was furious, but she was shouting my name because it was time to leave. Put your shoes on, bring a sweater. Come on, hurry up, in the early summer of 1978 you're not a little baby. I was not a baby, I was eleven years old and I hurried up. I climbed out of the wardrobe and went downstairs and stepped into my trainers and we left the house.

I can't have punched Nicky in the face for no good reason. I believe everything can be explained. Perhaps I felt threatened, and wanted to remind him I was older and stronger in the most direct way possible. I felt a need to strike him down, to cause him pain.

Nicky was extremely kind and helpful and a great conversationalist. He came to my room with a simple request or message, but before he could showcase his conversational skills I hit him. *Everything Nicky did he did well, be it sport, work, his music, or just kindness and good manners.* Let's see a good-mannered response to a punch in the nose, because everything you do you do well, like running away to your mummy. You squit, you blub-face crybaby. *We all remember Nicholas at the Barbecue as a bright handsome boy with a lovely sense of humor.*

Around the table at The Mill I had an opportunity to share the story of the punch. If I can remember it now I'd have remembered it then, but I wasn't planning to confess.

Not so stupid. Tough, yes: Nicky got that much right, one out of two, half-right in his judgment of his brother.

"He was really good at sport," I said, because it was my turn and I wanted to please. Safe start, but what next? What kind of things did people say to avoid raw feeling?

I said: "He was always generous in defeat."

What a lie that was. Then I couldn't go on. I choked back tears, then I was sobbing, racking my insides onto the table. The tears put an end to my charade, my search for the acceptable words. Nicky was not generous in defeat; he was a terrible loser, graceless and bad-tempered in defeat. The day after was far too soon for me to be saying what I felt expected to say in public, but under duress I gave it a go. Right from the start I was open to evasion and repression.

The Collected Letters of N. P. Beard amount to the following:

From: 25 Letters, 2 Postcards, 2 Easter cards, 1 Christmas card, 1 Birthday card.

To: 30 Letters, 21 Postcards, 10 Birthday cards, 3 Notelets.

I convince myself I have the material counted, categorized, under control. I have this many letters to and from, and no more, and I can study Nicky's collected letters in their controllable entirety. Three of them are in envelopes stamped with a first-class nine-pence Queen. She looks as unmoved as ever and fails to make eye contact, indifferent to the discovery that only one of Nicky's surviving letters is to me. Nicky is six years old, and understandably brief. I was eight and had already left home.

Dear Richard, How are you? Jeremy and I are very well. How do you like school? Love, Nicky.

He missed me terribly, but didn't know how to express his feelings. That's one interpretation. Another is that Mum sat him down and made him write a letter to reassure me at my new school that home life hadn't simply vanished. They weren't to know that it had, just as it would for Nicky two years later, supplanted by Victorian architecture and a jostle of boys tamed by intricate routines.

Nicky missed me terribly. I have no evidence that I ever wrote back.

At Pinewood School we had to write a weekly letter every Sunday morning, with strict formulas to guide us: the letters were checked for correct presentation to include margins, indents, and the appropriate sign-off. Senior boys should end letters to parents *Yours faithfully*. The younger ones, for a while, were allowed to continue to love.

In his letters from school, after he too left home, I search out Nicky's dreams: *For my birthday I would like an action man tank or a model or an encyclopedia and a chess set, please.* He provides me with objects I could use in that character questionnaire. Desires also reveal character, but Nicky wants what every boy wants, and expects to live to get it. Elsewhere, the letters are full of generalized observations, like a self-conscious historical novel: *This is the silver Jubilee year. I like it at this school.*

I learn that in rugby his position is scrum-half and which football team he supports — Mum writes: *Daddy says did you see Liverpool won!* For Mum, this is only one of a thousand exclamation marks. She hardly ever uses full stops, and her weekly letter to Nicky is bright and desperate with exclamations. It's as if Mum has discovered she can make her limited communication with her boys tremendously exciting, through punctuation. At this distance her relentless cheeriness feels forced and therefore sad.

Nice to see you on Sunday and Monday!! You are growing up! Soon be a teenager!! The exclamation marks are a visible response to our dispersed family, but my dad gives less of himself away. He is emotionally elusive behind his orthodox punctuation and illegible handwriting. *Keep trying*, he writes, whenever I can read him. *Keep trying and I am sure you will move up to top place.*

Nicky replies faithfully in blue Platignum ink, and like everyone he has problems spelling *eighth, Uncle, guard.* I sometimes want him to be more interesting as a correspondent than he is: *I have decided what to call the ginger teddy. I am going to call him Ginger.*

His letters are buoyant with goals scored and selection for that week's match. He enjoys his tests and his games, and every piece of news can be made competitive: *Is Jeremy*

*able to swim a width yet? If he can in the holidays I can chal-
lenge him to a race.*

Between the lines Nicky comes across as a buttoned-up
stoic, a small boy accepting the boarding-school conven-
tions that govern family relationships: *It was nice to see you
on Sunday, you looked very well.* This is the entire emotional
content of his letter in that particular week, a polite observation to his mother replacing the rough-and-tumble of
demonstrable homely love. Mum tries to respond in kind:
*We had a lovely weekend, didn't we? It won't be long now
until the Christmas holidays, it will be nice having you home.*

Mum betrays a constant longing to have everyone home,
but in the meantime appeals for feelings to be kept muted,
please, for everyone's sake: *It was nice to see you on Thursday, thank you for being big and brave and going into class,
it makes it better for when I come across.*

In both Mum and Dad's handwriting "Nicky" looks
sometimes like "Ricky," and vice versa, so I often can't be
sure if the letters are to him or to me. We are, in any case,
interchangeable. At the same school we wear identical
clothes, with the same basic timetable to our days, and
essentially each of these letters from home carries the same
silent message. From Mum, with the exclamation marks
deleted: *why the hell aren't you here? I miss you.* From Dad:
keep trying, it's for the best.

And so a pattern is established, of emotional lives
expressed in a language so reserved that sentiment is reduced

to shadow: *I am looking forward to getting your letter on Wednesday*. What is hidden may as well not exist. Nicky sends letters that read as if he wrote them in prison, begging for news of the outside world: *Please would you tell us (Timothy, Richard and I) who won the FA Cup?*

It was Ipswich, Nicky. I can look that up for you. Ipswich won the FA Cup final in May 1978, beating Arsenal by a single goal scored by Roger Osborne. You won't believe how football is going to change.

With hindsight, the postmarks on the surviving envelopes read like a countdown. 22 *Oct* 1977—he has nine months left. Please, before it's too late, somebody in these letters should understand the fragility of life and search for words of love. Nicky makes the first move. He experiments with how he signs himself off. *Love, Nicky or like Daddy calls me Nick Nack*. He signs off *love from Nickelpin*. He tries out *Nickpin* and *Nicholpin*. He insists on versions of himself more individualized than the minimal Beard minimus, and this reaching for an identity is part of his developing character. From *Nickypin* he gets to *Pinwin*. His thoughts evolve, the possibilities shift.

The routines, however, remain the same.

Thank you for coming to see me on Saturday. I am looking forward to seeing you on Wednesday.

He sees his mum and dad on Wednesdays and Saturdays because his life is measured out by sports fixtures. *Beard min soon put the Blues back into the lead and then went on to score his hat trick*. If Nicky wanted a regular meeting with his parents a competitive nature was essential, because parents were welcome to visit the school if they had a match to watch. They could admire from the sidelines, then a brief chat before showers and tea.

Football, rugby, cricket: to get selected for the team was to reunite the family. Nicky made all the teams. As did I.

I came first in a class of twelve boys.

Yes, and doing well at lessons was important too. His letters home are full of competition and standard presentation—the core values of boarding school. The inner workings of his nine-year-old mind remain obscure, except for the discovery that he's a reader. In his free time he reads *Lord of the Flies*. He knows that for boys unsupervised by adults, a punch in the face is only the beginning. He has read *Treasure Island*, in which an impetuous boy comes of age at the seaside.

I drive from The Mill back to the farmhouse at Tregardock. This time, after the twenty-minute walk through the gate, down the field, into the tunnel of gorse and toward the indented cliffs, I break out above the glory of Tregardock uncovered. The sand is vast and wide below me. The beach is suddenly exposed, unveiled, with none of the gradual reveal I'd have witnessed if I'd stayed the first time round.

I'm back. The day is cloudless, a summer breeze cooling me on the cliff and blowing flies off course from their scavenge of rabbit droppings. Now that the tide is out, surfers gather on the grass above the beach to peel themselves in and out of wet suits. I could cry, I feel like I could, but this time I'm not alone so I don't. Near the life buoy I sit on a promontory above the big brown beach and eat a biscuit. I can't say if this counts as emotional progress. I definitely don't want to be crying all the time, but I'll be disappointed if the beach breaks me up once and then never again.

I sit and I eat and I look. By my schoolboy reckoning, the beach is about 300 meters wide, a hard distance to gauge but somewhere between the longer Olympic sprint events. Out to the left are ten surfers surfing, like the early verse of a modernized song for Christmas. The surfers spend most of their time bobbing in the water and waiting, but today's Tregardock waves allow a surfer to stand up — I count the best of them — for 6 elephant, 7 elephant, almost 8 seconds. At low tide, about now, the coves have given way to a broad expanse of brown sand, dotted with uncovered outcrops of ancient rock.

Port Isaac is a fishing port adapted for tourism, but also the fictional village from the TV show *Doc Martin*. The Mill contains the past, but also a fresh layer of experience lived by Jim and Bertie Watson. Tregardock Beach isn't open to the same kind of change. It is what it naturally is, unaltered in a million years.

The tide turns back, and the waves hump in toward land. If I look closely enough — my mind flicking between then and now, between my inner knowledge and the visi-

ble scene—the rising sea will at some point exactly re-
create the landscape from our disaster in 1978. The beach
starts to diminish as the tide takes over; coves form and
they isolate patches of sand between rocks farthest out
toward the sea.

I climb down the cut-out steps beneath the life buoy. I'm
on the beach, on the sand. To the right, not that far away,
a cove forms. I go through a gap in the rocks and I'm on a
smaller beach. I find the spot, and look at it. I think this is
the spot. I know that memory can let me down in count-
less ways, but simple forgetting would be the biggest disappointment of all. I take photos to match against the past,
snapshots of the bare black eternal rocks. In theory, at the
right moment as the tide comes in, twice every twenty-
four hours, I should be able to snap identical views and
angles to those mapped in my memories.

I remember a narrow patch of sand a little farther to the
right than the main beach, where the waves were bigger on
the incoming tide. I'm looking for an area of sand free of
rocks, where two small boys can run into the sea and jump
rolling waves, then quickly lose track of their depth. Also,
the sides of the cove need somehow to prevent a rescuer
climbing along and leaping into the water to help a swimmer in trouble.

Geologically, meteorologically, the waves, rocks, sand,
wind, and light can converge as they did on 18th August
1978. At any other time, when Tregardock is marginally
different, the same event might not have happened, not in

the same way. A drowning couldn't happen right at this moment now, for example. At this stage of the tide at this time of day someone would notice a drowning boy. Surfers would come to the rescue, now that surfing in England exists.

A couple walk by, with their curious dog. They'd have saved a small drowning boy, these healthy young adults. I'd have treasured for the rest of my life the sunglasses of a braver, bolder type of bystander. Minutes earlier the undertow could have been weaker, and a few minutes later the beach would have disappeared, so we'd never have tried out the waves.

In this story so many factors are dependent on chance, or on fate. In September 1978 my dad wrote a letter of "observations" about Tregardock Beach, possibly with suggested changes for the benefit of future visitors. He needn't have bothered: with every passing minute I'm standing on a different beach. With every meter of approaching tide the topography and the hazards change.

I'm looking for 1978, feeling for my bearings by triangulating the reality of each perceptible moment against the geography of my memory. The roll of the waves comes back to me. We jumped and floated with the swell, weightless in every next surge of water. In comes the tide, and now this small portion of beach feels enclosed like a cove: the rocks are big if you're nine or eleven, and this is as close as I can get. The rocks, the sand, the liquid sea with shifting currents as fascinating as flames in fire, always changing, always the same. I am nearly in the right place. I sharpen my senses to the rawest memory prompts available — smells and sights and sounds. The emotion is somewhere here.

I touch rocks and a damp thatch of hyper-green sea-weed. I plead with the crash of waves and a lone drifting seagull to remind me. Please, for my own good. But maybe a perfect picture of the past depends on perfectly replicated conditions. A stream of freshwater rills through the sand to the sea, and to merge with 1978, at the age we were, I need the language we had for our experience. I know the words, because they fill Nicky's schoolbooks and letters, and we knew no other words but these. The sea was *hungry*. The air was *dusty*. The rocks *flint*. The sky was *kidnap*. These were the words we had.

To access a pure memory from the present I should wade into the water. I could wade right in, but can't face it, neither the cold nor the risk nor the drama. I don't want to enter the water. Instead, I find myself reenacting the running away. I hobble into a run, back toward the main beach, half on rocks and half on sand. From somewhere inside me rises a spontaneous mewling sound, a keening that squeezes through my chest, up into my tightened throat. I commune with the gulls, through my stiff unemotional jaw. The noise is because my leg hurts, that's what I tell myself. My leg hurts, and as I run I limp. I limp and run, and the wounded noise keeps rising and has nothing to do with my leg. The noise is inarticulate pain, grief that doesn't know how to express itself.

I run as far as the steps, climb up high above the beach, find a grassy spot where I lie down exhausted. I've finished the biscuits. I go to sleep, and when I wake not a trace of the beach remains, only gloss Atlantic Ocean from here to Nova Scotia.

2

18th August 1978

The Boy Will Die
The Boy Dies
The Boy Is Dead

The Boy Will Die

I'm the only eyewitness to the death itself, but not to the day, to the immediate before and after. There were others at Tregardock Beach on 18th August 1978. My brother Tim (13) was one.

He's alive, which allows us to get on well, and I've been seeing a lot of him recently in the photographs I salvaged from the attic. Christmas 1969, and in a professional studio Tim and I as toddlers get the matching Norwegian sweaters. Outside in the snow, also late Sixties, we each wear a bobble hat and hooded anorak, with shorts. Tough as they come.

At the beginning, in photographs, Nicky is just a baby in baby clothes. Then he gets a lesser pattern on his jumper, and parents have to be so very careful—from his unmatching clothes it can look like Nicky is excluded from the short-trousered tough-guy gang. In a slide from an early beach, Nicky is partially hidden by his big and greedy brothers, who have claimed the bucket and spade. We close in on the camera, demanding attention.

"There was a divide between the big boys and the little boys," Tim remembers.

As a grown man, fourteen months older than me, Tim has recently broken his leg—a stress fracture. We meet on a day of low, bumptious clouds, and he crutches himself to a bench where we sit beneath a tree to watch his Under-14 As play cricket. The pitch is sticky and slow, and the boys have trouble hitting the ball off the square.

"How did that divide show itself?"

"We got to stay up later. We could watch *Starsky & Hutch*, and Nicky couldn't. In the jobs. We had more chores to do. We were sometimes quite nasty to him."

"How exactly?"

"We made him fetch the ball when it went over the hedge," Tim says, "sent him round into next door's garden."

Nicky never grew big enough to do his share of the work, or for that matter to tell us to bog off and fetch the ball ourselves. He never drew level, as one day he surely would have done. We'd have compared A-level results and discussed house prices. I'd have drunk too much at his wedding and forgotten the birthdays of his wife and children.

I want Tim's version of 18th August 1978, and in my novels the older brother is invariably an impressive character who knows what's what. That's what older brothers are for, to show the way. Tim will have memories and opinions I respect, though I don't want to lead him with explicit questions. I want his memories pure, uncorrupted, free of influence from my visits to the attic and to Cornwall.

"I'm trying to retrieve as much of the day as possible," I say, "to help me gauge the impact of the event, not just on me, on all of us. The holiday setting seems important. We're on our summer holiday and supposed to be having a fabulous time."

Upstairs at The Mill, in the bedroom on the left, Tim wakes on 18th August 1978 in a bunk bed beside another bunk bed shared by me and Nicky. I'm on the bottom, which I must have chosen, because I'm older. Before anyone is up and about, Tim lies in his bed and attempts to clench his fists.

"It's true," he says. "It can't be done."

First thing in the morning, according to Tim, no one can make a hard, tight fist. He doesn't know why he remembers this, in connection with that particular day, but he does. Pure, uncorrupted. Otherwise we're on holiday, and it's another lovely morning under a blue Cornish sky. After breakfast we climb into the car, drive up the track and onto the road and from there we dream of the beach. In those days we saw so much more from the car than kids do now. No headrests to obscure the green fields, the stone cottages, the 1970s cars, every make of which we could identify from a distance by the design of the lights.

"At the beach the sun is shining," I say, forgetting that I

didn't want to prompt him, "the sea is blue. Then bam! —
from nowhere, catastrophe. Is that how you think it works?
We never again trust in simple happiness. Do you remember the holiday being perfect until that point?"

"I remember the beach, and being among those other
people."

What I know: the beach, the swelling waves, me and
Nicky out of our depth, the saltwater panic, thrashing back
in. The immediate family. There is so much I do not know.

"What other people?"

"Mum, who else was on this holiday, apart from us?"

"In the first week my parents came down."

Okay, I think, I'll fit them in later. "Where was Dad?"

"He had work. Mummy and Daddy left after the first
week, and then your other grandparents joined us. They
were with us when Nicky died. Your dad was there too. He
arrived during the second week."

I need to get these details straight, and confirmed by
reliable sources. I show Mum photographs on my phone
from my visit to The Mill.

"That isn't the right place," she says.

I scroll through the pictures: the façade of the house
from every angle, the gate from the lane, the timeless glass
panels in the kitchen door, and the original Belfast sink. I
have a photo of light in the dining-room window and the
split-ended stairs, and a photo of the unchanged bathtub.

"No, that's not it. It wasn't that nice."

"Mum, please, I'm not making this up."

Eventually she concedes that in 1978 the garden may have been overgrown, which is why she doesn't recognize it, but I can tell she's not convinced.

"The house wasn't painted white," she says, "nor the shutters green."

"They could have been painted later."

Mum thinks I'm making a mistake. Her maternal instinct is to protect me, because to her I'm always partly a child and therefore easily fooled. She worries about all of us this way, as if the universe is angled against us and only she knows how to save us from peril. Added to that, we have this new situation in which I've gone in search of the past. I have photos to prove the past exists, for real, but Mum is wary because she's the guardian of Nicky's flame, such as it is. Larger, smaller, any change in the heat or light will make her uncomfortable.

"We rented the house for four weeks," she says, correcting me. "My parents were with us in the first week. They left at the weekend, then Gran and Grandpa arrived. Tim's friend Guy Hake was there too. We had a full house."

"Mum."

Slow down, Mum. This is my life, yet I know so little. Mum is filling in the details, but I've already lost track. "Why did we book a holiday for four weeks? I thought we used to go for a fortnight?"

"That year was different. Your dad had cancer."

Your dad, as if whatever other faults he had, he was

always that—your dad. As far back as I can remember, Dad lived with the visible scars of a cancer, his neck scooped out at the back. Hospital consultants had carved away his neck to reveal shining tendons and nubs of white gristle, barely contained by a polished layer of thin healed skin. At first they gave him a curve of pink NHS plastic as a prosthesis, with some brown hair painted in at the top. He never wore it, but the plastic sat on his bedside table for months, possibly years.

"I spent the first week of the holiday on my own," Mum says, "with the idea of trying to cope without him. My parents came along to help with the house. That's another reason your dad wouldn't have wanted to be there."

Dad's cancer, in the form of his missing neck, became a distinguishing physical feature for the rest of his life. What I've forgotten is that the big surgical interventions must have happened around this time. It was another subject we never talked about.

The more patronizing condolence letters now start to make some sense. *You have been through so much in recent years, and have been so brave. Life just doesn't seem fair.* The earlier operations, before the cancer attacked again in 1978, also appear with characteristic restraint in the letters to Nicky at school. From Dad: *I am much better now*, and from Mum: *Daddy is very well, and will be home at the beginning of next week!!*, with progress reports thereafter: *Daddy is very well, and back at work!!*

"But he was there at the beach when Nicky died?"

I pull Mum back into 18th August. We have a practiced talent, I realize, for slipping away from contact with the day itself, in fact from any emotional disturbance. We do it automatically, with such expertise that no one need feel unsettled.

"Yes, he'd arrived in Cornwall by then. So had his parents, and Guy Hake, who was Timmy's friend."

First Mum's parents, then Dad's parents and a friend of Tim's from school. I know Guy Hake from the school magazines: *Captain of the School and Captain of the Greys.* That summer Hake had won the senior long jump, and on the cricket pitch his leg spin bowling *seemed to defy the laws of physics.* Here comes everyone on our annual family holiday, like a last-chance summer. My dad, with the cancer back in his neck again, was unlikely to make it to 1979. Mum was learning to distance herself, while the grandparents were seizing quality family time before the suffering truly started.

My mum's parents we rarely saw. My grandmother was a short fat woman with bandaged legs, something to do with water retention. Her surviving letter to Nicky has a plaintive tone, implying that obstacles have been established between us: *when you get time we would love to hear from any of you boys.*

As for my mum's father, he told exotic stories that favored narrative over veracity. Mum would cite as an example his wartime defiance of the Chinese People's Liberation Army on the Yangtze River. According to the story (as retold by Mum) my grandfather, the hero of HMS *Amethyst*, single-handedly kept the Chinese at bay. Which would represent an astonishing increase in his responsibilities, because in the attic we found his 1942 naval identity card: *Sick Berth Attendant, c/mx 52437.*

I never heard him tell this story myself, and it's possible that Mum's description of her father's exaggeration is exaggerated. Nevertheless, on my mother's side I have antecedents who confabulate, who are in need of fiction to improve on the facts.

On the Beard side, my dad's side, the grandparents were mostly robust. In 1978, at the age of seventy-three, my gran could easily have managed the path to Tregardock. My grandfather was seventy-eight, but probably felt younger because his own father was active and already 100. Both of them, on 18th August 1978, were capable of a bracing walk to the beach.

They were present at Tregardock on the day, just as Tim remembers, but I don't know at this stage how my dead grandparents can help advance the inquest. I know from condolence letters that earlier in the week they had taken charge of an outing— *Your welcome letter (and sweet smelling sachet) and its reference to taking Nicky and Jem off for a day seem so poignant now.*

Then I realize precisely how they can help. My grandfather was a keen amateur photographer. If he was at Tregardock, in the second week of our holiday, he'd definitely have taken his camera.

On the day itself, nobody paid sufficient attention to Nicky. Evidently, considering what happened. I can now rectify that error.

Once I started looking, I found more than 200 photos of Nicky as a baby and a boy. At an average shutter speed of 1/60th second, this adds up to nearly three and a half seconds of Nicky's life on Kodak paper and slides. Most of the prints I found loose in trunks and cardboard boxes in the attic, so my photo collection isn't quality-controlled. I have strange off-cuts, where Nicky's arm and chin appear at the edge of a frame, or he's in the background and out of focus. We may not have spoken about him, but no one could bear to throw him away. I have pictures of the back of his head, or most of his V-neck cable-knit sweater that I know is blue because I wore it the year before he did. Nicky appears in glimpses, in photos we wouldn't have kept of anyone else. These are secret, snatched rememberings—fragments that could neither be displayed nor discarded.

Then I have the formal photos from family occasions. These tell me little except that at certain times we were alive, and visibly bored. For my great-grandfather's 100th birthday, in April 1978, the camera work at the Post House Hotel off Junction 15 of the M4 was entrusted to a professional. Beatrice Ballard Photography of Swindon posed the fifty-one assembled family members in three tiers, like a school photo. Eight grandchildren, nineteen great-grandchildren—numbers that suggest the Beard gene pool could spare a single child.

My younger brother Jem sends me a box of slides, and even with expensive color transparencies, my grandfather snaps away with mixed results. In fact many of his photographs are terrible, overexposed or shadowed, with feet amputated or trees growing out of heads, like genetic family failings.

It doesn't matter. The dispersed photographs of Nicky have been gathered together, and I look at them with concentrated attention, as if each shot is a work of art. Circa 1977, and at a trestle table in the garden Nicky eats cold beef and celery sticks and what looks like summer pudding, and I want to shout him out of his contentment: "Don't eat! You're wasting your time!" Every sixtieth of a second carries him closer to death. He should be playing, laughing, running, to demonstrate—while he can—how he's utterly full of life.

Instead, the emotion that lumps in my throat is pity, because Nicky is so obviously marooned in his age. He wears brown sandals, and a nylon petrol-blue polo neck. His clothes are a particular disaster at special occasions, including a red-and-blue-striped waistcoat and for the 100th birthday party a red-checked shirt with a plain blue tie. I'm wearing the same, but I grew out of it.

I've had better bicycles than the Mini Moultons we're astride as we watch my uncle string up bunting for the

1977 Silver Jubilee. God, those were awful bikes for children, though Nicky will never find out that putting Marlboro stickers on the down-tube won't make them any cooler.

The photographs overrepresent holidays: Nicky on trains and in fishing boats, but mostly at the beach. From 1972 onward (dates and places in pencil on the back of the prints) I have a disproportionate number of images showing Nicky running out of a shallow sea toward the camera. Ergo, according to the surviving pictorial evidence, he died doing what he loved. He's in the sea on holiday—we all are—fighting the tide with buckets, clawed fingers, every available weapon, digging trenches and building ramparts, four boys together raising hilariously ineffective defenses against nature.

I study every picture. The photographs cut through a major obstacle to feeling, which is my acceptance until now that Nicky's only role in life is to be dead. He is the dead brother, true for so many years it might as well always have been so, but the comfort of "always" is dissolved by the photographic evidence.

All Nicky's life is here: he crawls, sits, splashes in the bath with his new baby brother, grows into a toddler with a middle manager's round face, dark hair coming in taking the same male pattern shape as hair going out. His tricycle, his seventh birthday, Stonehenge, the paddling pool out the back on a sunny day, full snorkel-diving in ten inches of Great Barrier Reef. He just is. He lives.

I was desperate to block out my images of Nicky in the sea, but the death scene would not stay suppressed—the undertow, his clamped mouth, the terror. I tried harder until, to be absolutely certain, I wiped out all memory of Nicky as a person. The scorched earth of repression starts to look like a poor life's work.

So concentrate. See him how he was, how in these photos he always will be: playing cricket in the garden, a spoked Austin 7 wheel as the wicket, in full kit including pads and a cap and neatly rolled sleeves like Geoffrey Boycott. Nicky has an easy batting stance, and a strong forward defensive. He poses the follow-through of an on-drive, the hardest shot in the book, his polyarmored Slazenger held high and his eyes following the ball toward an imaginary boundary. I have this picture of his dreams.

One photograph I find ignites a memory. Wales, one summer a couple of holidays before 1978, and four brothers in anoraks have been arranged on a disused metal railway bridge. Black and white. Nicky is in front and to the right, nearest the camera, kneeling and pretending to unfasten a rivet on a girder, as if he's an engineer. Everyone is looking at the camera except me and him. Nicky is attending to his rivet and I'm looking at Nicky, but slyly, face to the camera but eyes sliding meanly to the right. I want to hide my spiteful sideways eye on whatever it is he's doing, but the photo has caught me out. I remember now. I hate Nicky's pretending. It's only for a photograph and you should know, actually, that he's not a qualified engineer.

If my grandfather had been a better photographer this image wouldn't have survived—he'd have taken a picture with everyone smiling happily, faces to the front. As it is, I have slitted eyes viciously angled to the right, and I am despising the pretensions of my younger brother with a passion. He should be facing the camera like the rest of us. On this particular day I look an evil little bastard, as captured on film, blown up and mounted on card and displayed for a long time above my grandparents' fireplace.

That nasty look, and the feeling behind it, wasn't an isolated incident. In another photo Nicky is "running" out of the sea, but I know for a fact he's not. He's standing still, only pretending to run. He's "mending" his upturned bicycle, only he doesn't know the first thing about bike mechanics. He's eight. What he's actually doing is drawing attention to himself, making sure he's the one in the photo. I resented his showing off, his attention-seeking. As witnessed on the bridge in Wales, I was hyperalert to his ploys.

I look at these photos of him pretending to be what he's not, and feel the echo between my anguish then and my emotions now. Acting out his mechanics, or hamming up his exit from the sea, Nicky is imagining what the picture might look like and he in it, up on a prominent mantelpiece. He is making calculations about the future, deliberately furthering his interests. He is fully conscious and has a mind of his own.

The horror. He has started to demonstrate that *he has a character.* Always I've struggled to accept him as a self-aware and independent human being, not just now, but even at the time. Nicky, you're a little boy who belongs with other little boys. *I'm* one of the big boys. Your growing up is not in my best interest.

In the Swindon attic I found a 1970s packet of commercially developed photographs. The paper wallet was unusual in itself, because my grandfather had his darkroom where normally he developed his own photos, though not these. *Your color prints on Kodak paper, By Max Spielmann. The Specialist Photo Printer. Liverpool—Birkenhead—Wallasey—Chester.*

Places far from home. I opened the packet. Inside, first in the stack of thirty-six prints, is Nicky on the beach in color. On Tregardock Beach, unmistakably aged nine, sitting on a Tregardock rock. There he is, hugging his knees and gazing out to sea, looking for the magic seventh wave. Given the second-week arrival of my grandparents, and the rarity of an outing to Tregardock, this is a photograph from the day itself, 18th August 1978, and that is definitely him.

I had not been expecting this.

Nicky is a good-looking boy, a red-and-yellow striped towel over his knees and a thin silver chain round his neck. He's glorious, beautiful. I uncovered one new print after another. At the beginning of the day he's wearing trunks and a tracksuit top—navy blue with two white stripes down the arm and an octagonal *GO* patch sewn on the left front panel.

Then he's in the blue Kodacolor sea, for the first time that day, along with Dad, Mum, and Tim. Above them, some frivolous white cloud. I don't want to be as close as these photographs bring me. I do, I really do. The surprise of these images, and their freshness, carries me in tight to the real thing, to the experience not the story.

On his last day alive Nicky wears swimming trunks. The family plays cricket on the beach. Nicky is in bat, and he's about to leap down the wicket to Dad's bowling as Dad winds up his horrible overarm action. I have the day itself in color pictures, not mocked up by fallible memory. This game of beach cricket in the sunshine of 18th August 1978 is a true story. Look, in the background, the waves that day are not so big. Beyond the breakers there is a flat, flat sea.

Jem wears striped trunks, a white Adidas T-shirt, and a Mr. Men pendant. I bring out the magnifying glass, but can't make out exactly which Mr. Man. Nicky sometimes wears a red celluloid visor attached to a white toweling headband, and the pendant on the chain round his neck is Snoopy.

I have blue trunks and wet hair. I've already been in and out, and have nothing to fear from whoever's splashing me from outside the margins of the photo. Nor do I have any shyness in front of the camera. Bring it on. I am eleven and immortal, and I know it.

My dad's skin is an English white. He has cancer, so probably doesn't much care about his tan. Also, there's hardly anyone on the beach to see us. We have the place to ourselves. Guy Hake, in blue trunks and shapely head-boy pectorals, chases Tim through the shallows. Gran sits fully clothed in skirt and cardigan on a tartan picnic blanket. We the children have rakes, spades, blue wooden sailboats, all the sand and sea we need. We embark on major excavations.

"It was a perfectly ordinary day," Mum says. "I'd packed rolls for lunch, and fruit."

Tim's trunks are quartered in blue and white, and early on he takes charge of the bat and the football. Even Grandpa is wearing his trunks, but also a white short-sleeved shirt, though I keep coming back to Nicky. At the beach I keep my eye on him — he runs, a balanced runner, with the leanness for speed over middle distances, 800 meters, a mile. Nicky laughs, Nicky thrashes Jem hands-down in a sprint race.

I wish he wouldn't smile so much, making what's about to happen even worse. Stop smiling. You don't know, you don't know.

My grandfather has wasted half his thirty-six shots by taking photos earlier in the week, of a dinghy race, and a postcard view of Port Isaac. Idiot. He has snapped Gran at The Mill playing French cricket with a blue plastic bat and a red rubber ball. Sweet, but still a waste. Then he remembers, no, he respects a premonition and saves half the roll for Tregardock and the capture of Nicky's last day, Nicky's last turn at bat. No one else, just Nicky, poised for a healthy thwack at my dad's filthy bowling. Later, at rest in a blue roll-top sweater, in the honeyed light, Nicky looks unbearable, miraculous.

At the time of this photograph he has about an hour, perhaps two, left to live. He was growing up, changing, and of all his days this was the day he was most himself. The day after he'd have been more of himself again. Guy and Tim play together in the pictures—they're the big boys now. Jem is younger and belongs with his mum, but look at me. Look at me now. I'm not a baby. I'm in the middle with Nicky, and not scared of anything.

One of us, Nicky or I, asks for a last swim, as if to prove that we too are the big boys: confident, independent, deserving of special dispensation. Of course no one goes swimming alone, but we'll be together, the two of us, me and Nicky, with the implication that we'll each look out for the other. On the far side of a big rock is a patch of sand with better waves. Come on, hurry because the tide's coming in and the sand will soon be gone. A last tilt at the waves, since we're here. Come on, hurry up, before it's too late.

The Boy Dies

The commercially developed photos, sent away to Liverpool, are a record of what happened last. So what happened next?

In the novel *Lazarus Is Dead* I invented a younger brother for the biblical character Lazarus. I called him Amos, and I drowned him in a made-up version of Lake Galilee, I suspect to try and kill the memory — better out than in. The ploy failed. Instead, shaping Nicky's death as fiction released years of pent-up, stubborn denial. My unconscious mind had been stalking this nonfiction event for some time — I'd been closing in, then veering away, testing the pain, attempting to treat the wound with fiction.

When I drowned Amos, fiction and memory started to merge. In the novel Lazarus is in the water but unable to save his brother, and the portrayal of what happened next is recognizably founded on what I remember — the furious paddling, the treacherous footing, the abandonment. The novel is, however, a story, because I do like to tell myself stories, if they'll help.

Lazarus Is Dead was published on 18th August 2011, but the anniversary of the date was a coincidence. Or was it? The date of publication was outside my control, and at the time had no particular significance for me, because I hadn't yet taken an interest in the date of Nicky's death. Nevertheless, I expected a reaction from my family: for the first time, one of my books contained a public retelling of our true life-changing event. No one reacted.

I'd assumed the family lived with the same basic memory of Nicky's drowning. But if we did, nobody wanted to talk about the Amos story in *Lazarus Is Dead* and my almost-accurate recall of Nicky's final seconds of life. Perhaps no one recognized the drowning for what it was. I'd forgotten, along with so much else, that I was the only person who had this close-up knowledge, which I'd never previously shared.

For me, fiction was a way of owning up, belatedly, to what only I knew. I hadn't stayed in the water to rescue my brother. I'd failed to look out for him, and the novel was an outlet for this memory with the built-in defense that not every word was true: I made up some horsing around that delays Lazarus noticing how Amos is in trouble. I also allowed Lazarus two attempts to save his brother. Part of my initial intention, I think, was to build a new obstacle between me and 1978, using fiction to replace what did happen with what didn't.

Instead, the act of writing floated these memories to the surface. Perhaps there *was* some horsing around, and I did try twice to push Nicky toward the shore. I don't know.

What I do know is that the fiction wasn't entirely successful. The strain shows. The drowning passage is flawed because the setting is a lake and lakes don't have undertows, at least I suspect not, however biblical a storm can get in Israel. I didn't bother to check whether the underfoot gravel of Lake Galilee drags back out like the sand at Tregardock Beach. The greedy rip makes much more sense on the North Cornwall coast, because that's where it's true. The past has its definite place.

I don't speak with my younger brother Jem all that often. We have a Nicky-sized hole that separates us, making the five-year age gap feel wider than it is. If I'm the second of the big boys, Jem is the second of the little boys, and after Nicky dies he's little and alone.

On a rare occasion when he's visiting down south, I prize Jem away from the boy-girl-girl-boy arbitration required by his four children under the age of six. We escape to an English green space, an expanse of mown grass bordered by trees, a church spire in the distance, and the comforting sound, in the twenty-first century, of traffic not too far away.

"Tell me what you remember."

Jem remembers a dog falling off a wall, "Clea or the gray one, it cracked its head." Of the house itself, he remembers the sound in the overhead wires as the wind blew down the valley. "We had transparent blue visors, and Nicky had a stain on his that Grandpa removed."

The visors are red, as I know from the packet of color photos. I have been collecting evidence, and now that I'm paying proper attention I can see the distortion in Jem's remembering. The dog fell off the wall on our holiday to the same house in the same place, but the previous year. I have a letter from the owner settling the 1977 electricity bill, which proves that we were there. As were the dogs. In 1978 no dogs, or none in the photos I can date by T-shirts. In 1977 I'm wearing University of South Carolina, which in 1978 has passed down the line to Nicky. Jem is merging the two years into one.

At other times his memories aren't wrong, not exactly, but they differ from mine. These variations emphasize the distance between us, because as a family we've never spoken enough to agree a story. We haven't collaborated on acts of recollection, so our memories exist in isolation. In some ways this allows each of us a more direct encounter with the past—we remember what we remember, our independent memories unvarnished by sharing and retelling. On the other hand, memories that have warped, possibly for reasons of self-protection, can evolve unchallenged. Denial makes this divergence possible.

"I still have the Mr. Men pendant I wore that summer," Jem says. "There's something wrong with it. It's the shape of Mr. Greedy, but it should be purple. It could be Mr.

Dizzy, but the color and shape don't match. I've checked the back of the books. My pendant could be Greedy or Dizzy, but it's neither. I don't know who it's meant to be."

All through that summer Jem wore a pirated Mr. Men pendant, close but not the real thing. He can picture Nicky's pendant, and the fine silver-colored chain. He thinks Nicky had a Snoopy. We agree the story, and anyway I've seen the pendant in a photograph, up close under a magnifying glass. Snoopy, the dog from *Peanuts*, without a doubt.

In his house Jem had been storing a significant stock of photos, the two boxes of our grandfather's slides that he'd kindly sent me for inspection. I ask him how he came to have them.

"I asked for them. They were going to be burned."

He also has a framed print that Gran used to keep on her bedroom wall, of him and Nicky bursting out of sandy blocks on a sprint up an unknown beach.

"I believe this is the last photo," Jem says. It might be, taken with one of my grandfather's many cameras. Always racing, right to the end. It fits, and this is the version according to Jem.

"How did you get hold of it?"

Unbidden, I have an insight into how Mum must feel. Nicky used to be her territory, but now I've decided he's mine. I'd prefer Jem not to have taken an interest, but he evidently has.

"I asked for that, too."

The running photo is on the top shelf in the toy room of his new house that I've never visited. Nicky and Jem in the sand is next to a photo of Dad, and another of Jem's first child as a baby. This is the past that Jem has chosen to exhibit.

"What do you think happened on the day Nicky died? I appreciate you were only six, but any memory you have. When you tell the story, what do you say?"

"I don't."

"To your wife, for example. You must have told her something about it?"

"Nicky was swept out to sea and he drowned."

Our exchange is a mismatch because I'm prepared. I'm several months' cold with research. I've had my shocks, my feelings, but also long experience of putting them aside. "You use that phrase to tell the story? He was swept out to sea and he drowned."

"Yes."

"That's what you say, but it's vague. How was Nicky swept out to sea?"

Jem looks at me. He has a talent for silence, of the kind that asks me to hear the echo of what I've just said. His silence also acts like a challenge; whoever speaks next is the loser.

"There must be more," I say, "even in this version. He was swept out to sea and he drowned. How did that happen? There's no context, no story."

"He was walking along the seafront and he was swept out to sea and he drowned."

"Not sure that makes much sense. He walks along and gets swept out. Have you ever known anything like that to happen? I mean to anyone else you know, in all the years since? Is that something you normally worry about, when you take a walk at the seaside?"

Memories can evolve, and over time lose contact with the true original events. We develop adaptations of the day. Nevertheless, Jem also has what he calls "physical memories," and we agree on what he means—an intense visceral connection with specific moments around Nicky's death that feel lived and immutable. These constitute vivid memories of the day that no amount of repression or evasion will budge.

"I remember hiding behind a rock."

Despite that, Jem can almost believe he wasn't at the beach at all. "I couldn't tell you where I was. I feel really empty, but I had to be there somewhere. I wasn't with a childminder."

We obscure the calamity in our different ways. Jem has turned to logic to explain the wasteland of his memory— if he doesn't remember, then he can't have been there. And if he wasn't there, aged six, logic invents the services of a childminder to explain his absence. Jem constructs a narrative that makes sense, its only weakness being a total lack of truth. I track back to where I started the inquest, my barometer for measuring levels of denial, and ask Jem if the date is something he has in his head.

"I know it's the summer, and where it happened, Port Isaac. I don't know where it fits in my life. I don't know what happened. Do you know what happened?"

I find I'd prefer not to say. I'm jealous of my knowledge of Nicky in the water that day, and I like being the only one to know. I've resisted and repressed the memory, but by doing so I've protected my status as the person most intimately involved. This information is mine, and makes me special.

Jem repeats the question three or four times. "Do you know what happened?"

"I was in the water with him."

That's the story I tell.

"You were swimming?"

This matters to Jem. His gray-green eyes are unblinking, and I realize he genuinely doesn't know—that no one does but me.

"Were you in the sea swimming?" he asks again. Now he's the one cold with curiosity and I'm the brother who's flustered.

"We were."

But I don't want to tell that story now, of what I know. As if I don't yet know enough to be certain. I worry that each retelling might soften the edge of the memory, when the sharpness needs safeguarding for the emotional awakening I thought I wanted.

*

I say: "Just tell me about the day." I never know what I'm going to get, first from Jem and now from Tim. "The actual day when he died."

"Was it the second year we'd been there?" Tim isn't sure.

"Maybe. There was a holiday when a dog fell off a wall."

Until the summer of 1978, the worst we'd suffered on holiday was a dazed dog. On the morning of 18th August, as he remembers it, Tim wakes up and tries to clench his fists. We're having this chat midafternoon on an outside bench, no Internet, no quick way of checking the facts about fists, but for Tim in his bed that early August morning, in The Mill near Port Isaac, nothing bad has yet taken place. The day moves on. Next he remembers sitting on the beach at Tregardock, watching people come down the steps cut into the rock at the end of the path. To no one in particular he says: "Those people haven't read their tide tables."

The tide must have been coming in, as it was when Nicky drowned. Tim's mind has preserved a moment from not long before. He is thirteen and the tide table is important to him—he likes to understand the workings of the world. He wants to get life right, but the value of knowing stuff is about to diminish. He nails the truth about tides, of when it is good and right to arrive at the beach and when it is not. His command of the facts will make no difference.

"One of the boys is in trouble."

Tim's first contact with the catastrophe.

Someone says, "*One of the boys is in trouble.*" I press him on this quoted line of direct speech, but he doesn't know who said it, when or where—the words exist unattached, isolated.

"One of the boys is in trouble."

In reply, back on the beach, Tim says: "Guy can help. He's a very strong swimmer."

At Pinewood School, Guy Hake is *Captain of the Greys and Captain of the School,* information verified by the school magazine. He has blue trunks and proper muscles, but I've looked up his sports-day results and Tim is wrong. Hake places third in the senior sprints and second in throwing a cricket ball, but is absent from the podium at the swimming gala. Swimming isn't his thing.

"Did you know I was in the water?"

"I knew you were together."

He can't say how he knows this. I suppose I could have told him on some earlier occasion, but our project of denial has been a lifetime's work, a going concern. He could just as easily have remembered it, but never have said so.

"Why did we never talk about this? We never have, have we?"

"I try to give Mum a phone call near his birthday," Tim says. "Around March the twenty-third."

I'm surprised—Tim never forgot Nicky's birthday. Briefly, I worry that the hard-core denial has been mostly mine. The others chat about Nicky behind my back, at least once a year. I test Tim out with my pivotal original question, but no, he can't date with certainty the day of Nicky's death. You too, Tim. Nor can he recall the name of the beach.

"I wouldn't even recognize a picture," he says. "It's black."

"Blank? You mean the rest is a blank.".

"Not blank," Tim says. "Black. It's black."

We invest faith in the facts of the world so as not to be fooled by fictions. We crave the news, daily, to be sure of what's happening—to know is to feel prepared, and protected. This is the way things really are.

From some deep BBC archive I had hoped to unearth the TV news bulletin that brought the fact of Nicky's death to the people of Swindon. Several of the commiseration letters dated 19th August refer to a news bulletin—*The evening news tells us of this terrible tragedy*, and the local angle makes it perfect content for *Points West*, the regional roundup that follows the *News at Six*. I contact *Points West*, still going strong, to ask if they have archive material from August 1978.

No one can tell me. The interns on the phones have trouble understanding the year 1978 as a believable concept, because *Points West* is a news program, exclusively concerned with what's new. Do I have anything new to tell them? I do not, or not in the sense they mean. I have plenty of old news, discovered for the first time.

The death was also covered extensively in print, which led to *the shock we all felt in reading of the tragic death of Nicholas.* The soonest a newspaper could have carried the story was the early edition of Saturday, 19th August, and I can check who said what at the British Library in London. **Newspapers** is on the second floor, round the corner from **Humanities** 2. Anyone with a reader's card can drop by the library on Euston Road and ask the helpful staff (Alice, in this instance) to call up the printed news of any single day. The press will have taken a view, producing material I can try to align with memory and interviews and formal documentation.

At the same time, as I'm waiting for my requests to emerge from the vault, I worry about the consequences of doing too much research. The information I've gathered so far has prized open memories grown closed, but other people's opinions soon pile up. I don't want to crush my personal and precious connection to an afternoon in 1978 under the weight of dusty paperwork. I have memories that exist independent of the public record, but I'm still pleased that newspaper editors seized on our family disaster. N. P. Beard was famous for a day—he made it into the papers.

The Evening Advertiser, Swindon, Saturday, August 19, 1978, *Final Edition.* The *Swindon Adver* leads with the story, a front-page headline in full-caps lock:

Holiday Horror
BOY, 9
SWEPT
TO HIS
DEATH

After a hard week's work, readers of the Swindon *Evening Advertiser* want full-on sentiment. *A nine-year-old Swindon boy has been drowned in a holiday tragedy. Little Nicholas Beard was knocked over by four-feet waves, then dragged into the surf at low tide — while his parents were relaxing nearby on the Cornish beach.*

The disinformation begins, for the sake of a dramatic story — the waves and the low tide are wrong; the *little* plucks at Swindon heartstrings while the tragically unaware parents — the pathos — are *relaxing* nearby. This is the news, today and every day: do not dare relax.

Nicholas was playing with a group of children at the water's edge. No he was not, and I should know. *Nicholas was knocked over by waves and lost in the surf. His body was later spotted floating in the sea.*

Nicky's death, as news, is ridiculous. He's *lost* in the surf, in some way his playmates from that useless group of imaginary children don't notice. Plot hole, a pause, then he's floating and dramatically spotted. Now here come the belated uniformed heroes: *Port Isaac inshore lifeboatmen rescued Nicholas and gave the kiss of life, but he apparently was already dead.*

The *Western Evening Herald* (Saturday, 19th August)

isn't more reliable — *The Port Isaac inshore lifeboat was on the scene within minutes*. On Monday, the *Western Daily Press* identifies the grieving family as residents of Balmoral Crescent, Swindon, an address that doesn't exist — **Holiday boy, 9, drowned by wave.**

The newspapers do little to clarify the sequence of events. A later account, in the *Sunday Times* of 27th August, is an end-of-season review of summer deaths, and the national paper makes more of an attempt to find out why.

"We're getting many foreign visitors now," says district councilor Ian McWatt. *"Most of them come from inland areas in Europe and have no idea of the danger of the sea."*

On reflection, a month after Nicky drowned, the Beard family from inland Swindon acted as naively as foreigners; yes, as stupidly as that. In the *Herald* the pilot of the rescue helicopter, Flt. Lt. John Mabbot, is less of an anti-European. He blames non-Cornish people, wherever they come from: *Most of the incidents are due to holidaymakers just not appreciating how dangerous this stretch of coastline is…Holidaymakers do not seem to realize how quickly the tide advances in this area.*

Newspapers love to incriminate, and children die in the waters off Cornwall because their parents are ignorant tourists. But as so often in England, the fault may also lie with *Britain's general bad weather pattern this year.*

Surf Boy Is Fourth Victim.

The "Surf Boy" headline in the *Western Morning News* summons images of a glistening athletic teenager, as the subeditor well knows. The truth is less delectable: Nicky was a scrawny nine-year-old boy in blue trunks that were slightly too big for him. That's the reality. When it comes to the facts, journalists can be plain wrong: *None of the victims was in the sea; all were washed from rocks.*

Often newspapers seem informative, unless a reader is familiar with the material, at which point journalism can feel approximate and superficial. With Nicky's story, some papers are more accurate than others. *The boy was playing in the surf when powerful Atlantic waves knocked him down. A fierce undertow swept him out to sea* (*Western Evening Herald*, 19th August 1978).

That description fits most closely with what I remember, perhaps because the local reporters would have interviewed witnesses and taken statements. They'd have asked the people who were there, and I can do the same.

The Royal National Lifeboat Institution archive in Poole provides a single-spaced list of Port Isaac lifeboat callouts between 1968 and 1980. A page and a half of them, with the typewriter ribbon fading toward December 1971. During this period the boat launches between five and twelve times a year, and by far the busiest months are July and August, the holiday season. The RNLI typist has bashed each mission onto the page in its shortest possible form:

1975 *Oct. 5 Cattle fallen from cliff, stood by.*
1977 *Jul. 17 Skin diver, saved.*

Most callouts end happily. The Inshore Inflatable Lifeboat at Port Isaac saves dinghies and dories and yachts. The volunteer crews stand by for canoes and motorboats, while ensuring that daydreamers cut off by the tide have a scare and not a catastrophe. A surprising number of walkers need assistance after falling from the cliffs. I'm not quite sure how that happens, but it does, or did.

On 14 August 1978, four days before the callout for Nicky, *Two persons in the sea, saved.* Yet on Friday 18th August, despite the valuable experience gained on the Monday, *Recovered the body of a bather.* Karen Harris, the RNLI archivist, has helpfully highlighted the entry. I read in black and white, and now fluorescent yellow, that the boy has become a body. The body of a bather. A new source, the same information. Denial is futile.

The RNLI station in Port Isaac sits in the hinge of the village's V, shops and houses mounting the slopes on either side. Facing the slipway to the beach and harbor, with its fishing boats and careening gulls and solid storm walls, the lifeboat station is at the center of what Port Isaac has always been about: the junction of land and sea.

On the day I visit, the lifeboat is secure on its trailer in the station, meaning the seas between Polzeath and Tintagel are currently free of incident. The lifeboat station is effectively a large shed, only a couple of feet wider on either side than the sixteen-foot boat that fills it. I squeeze past, toward the office at the back, and take in the posters pinned to the walls: *Swimming—swim at a lifeguarded beach, between the red and yellow flags.* The walls also carry plenty of information about the D-class lifeboat itself, and I learn that its inflatable orange sides are called sponsons. This modernized semirigid craft is an update of earlier versions, slightly more powerful, but otherwise similar to the boat in service in 1978. I run my hand along a sponson. The man-made material feels tough, fast, serious. Orange.

The glass-fronted office at the back of the shed is the control room, where I've arranged to meet Chris Bolton, the Port Isaac RNLI operations manager. Chris has invited along the volunteer press officer, Bob Bulgin, who lives in the village and does more than promote the lifeboat service—if the news is bad, Bob tells me, he's on hand to process the information, not the emotion. At last, I think, my dream job. The RNLI is a voluntary organization, reliant on locals, so Chris and Bob both know Ted Childs, who lives round the corner and crewed the lifeboat in 1978.

"On my specific day?" I'm astonished. They've found someone who was directly involved. "Are you sure? Was he actually in the lifeboat on the eighteenth of August?"

"Yes. We asked him about it." Chris has swiveled his command chair away from the radios and radar equipment. He gives me his full attention. "Ted remembers the day well."

Unfortunately, Ted Childs is at the dentist.

"He was actually in the lifeboat?"

"He calls the shout a nasty one. Very nasty. When he spoke about it, I saw he was shaken."

Chris Bolton knows I'm here because of Nicky (in hard RNLI type: *1978 Aug 18. Recovered the body of a bather*), but there's a limit to what he can tell me because he wasn't there. And this isn't 1978. These days, partly because of wet suits and better general awareness of ocean dangers, the lifeboat responds to fewer incidents. Even in 1978, most families on holiday in Cornwall had a smashing fortnight and left the county without anyone dying.

At first, in the operations room, we make lifesaver small talk about bodies. Port Isaac has a dummy for practice rescues called "Dead Harry," but Chris tells me I'm right, sometimes the body is never recovered. Gases in a drowned corpse can create sufficient buoyancy to enable drift in underwater currents. If the body sweeps past the natural barrier of Tintagel Head, it can disappear far into the Atlantic and may never be seen again.

"In 1978, from Tregardock, how would they have called the lifeboat?"

I'm back on track. All I want, really, is to know about Nicky's last day.

"Someone would have run to the farm," Chris says. He knows all the beaches along the coast, and the houses at the end of lanes nearest the sea. "They'd have asked Mrs. Thom at the farmhouse to phone the coast guard. I'd say that would take at least ten minutes, at best. She's dead now."

"And once someone gets in trouble," I push on, "how long do they usually have?"

Chris doesn't say "body," he says "casualty." A swimmer is never "drowning," but "in difficulties." The length of time a person can survive in the water depends on body-mass and the clothes they're wearing, and how well they can swim.

"There's no fixed rule. We had a case at New Year where a man kept himself alive for forty-five minutes. Though in your brother's case, hypothermia wasn't a problem."

Death by drowning can happen quickly, Chris says, in less than a minute. I remember it as quick. I have my memory and now some context: Mum keeps an eye on Jem and shakes out the dregs from the Thermos. Tim splashes in the shallows with Guy Hake. Dad, what? No idea. I'm out of sight and in the sea with Nicky. He starts to die, so very quickly, and I feel the fight-or-flight certainty that I too will soon be drowning. I fight the undertow and flee the danger. I do both, anything, everything.

Chris puts the kettle on. Bob gives me a handful of leaf-lets, and to defer these feelings of panic and reawakened grief I skim through lifeboating facts, finding solace in the RNLI's organized defiance of dangers at sea: the Port Isaac lifeboat can launch into surf up to seven feet high, and a lifeguard can swim 200 meters in three and a half minutes; 140,000 lives have been saved since 1824, and 325 from Port Isaac since the station reopened in 1967. Excellent work, I think. One more wouldn't have hurt.

Or more than one, because 400,000 people drown annually worldwide, 50 percent of them children. They can't all be victims of fate. Every year, even now, about 150 people drown in the UK. Compared to deaths on the road, that's not so many, but drowning kills more UK citizens than cycling accidents. The figures are slightly distorted by suicide—no one commits suicide by riding a bike.

The most recent callout for the Port Isaac lifeboat was in response to an abandoned car on the cliffs, a note visible on the dashboard. Out sped the lifeboat, but in vain, because the suicidal driver was later spotted in a Wade-bridge pub. He'd changed his mind.

Chris comes back with mugs of tea. I ask him what he thinks happened in 1978. "How do people actually drown?" I ask.

"They take a mouthful of water and panic. With sea-water there's also a risk of secondary drowning."

Inhaled seawater is absorbed into the lungs, which damages the membranes needed to exchange oxygen and carbon dioxide. After an apparent recovery a person can drown hours later, nowhere near any water. "It doesn't happen that often," Chris says, "but it's always a danger."

"I'm fairly sure Nicky drowned the first time round."

"You should talk to Ted Childs," Chris says. "He was in the boat. You can see he still feels deeply about it."

At the mention of feeling, I find another question: "Why aren't there lifeguards at Tregardock?"

Dad's letter of observations (whatever it said) hadn't

roused the District Council to tame the wild allure of Tregardock Beach: no lifeguards then, none in evidence now.

"The spot is too remote," Chris says, "and the beach accessible only at low tide. We have plenty of safe beaches elsewhere."

Like sheltered Port Gaverne, for example, a short walk from Port Isaac harbor and a natural fortress against the worst of the Atlantic. Port Gaverne is a safe place for children to play, and a beach we knew because it features in that last packet of photos.

I show Chris the 1978 cutting from the *Sunday Times* about killer waves:

Bank holiday visitors to north Cornwall face a new peril this year. Rogue waves, born hundreds of miles out in the Atlantic, have swept four holiday-makers to their deaths in the past month, and there are fears that more fatalities may follow.

Sunday Times, 29th August 1978

"There is no such thing as a freak wave," Chris says. "They're quite common. What people don't understand is the speed of the tide."

At which point the phone rings, and I'd love to see Chris and Bob spring into lifesaving action. But instead of an incident, on the other end of the line is retired RNLI crewman Ted Childs. His appointment with the dentist finished earlier than expected, he's at home and he could drop by right now, if anyone's interested. His house is a two-minute walk from the lifeboat station.

So far Dad hasn't featured in anyone's memory of the day: he's absent from my version and from Mum's and from Tim's, though he was with us that day at Tregardock. I have the cricket photograph to prove it, and parents are the fifth emergency service, the in-house 999. They're supposed to rapid-response their children's cries for help.

By 1978 it was common knowledge that Dad wouldn't be succeeding his grandfather into the pages of *Guinness World Records*. The tumor in the back of his neck had expanded and twisted round the top of the vertebrae, and was now reaching toward the cells of the brain. Mum remembers the hospital surgeon, an Egyptian, describing two possible outcomes to surgery. The knife might cut out the cancer, and Dad would live, though he'd wear a neck brace for the rest of his life.

"If we get it all."

But if the scalpel failed to slice deeply or precisely enough, perilously close to bone and cartilage, Dad would die. This was the third major operation on his neck and his last chance—a final attempt before he had no neck left on which to operate.

Dad's medical records would confirm the details, but the family doctor tells me by phone that the records are lost. All I have is a medical file from Dad's study, but the dates are too late, only a couple of years before he died. He had a lot wrong with him, by the end, even without historical procedures described as *tissue removed from spinal cord at least 35 years ago.* The consequences remain worth noting: *neck movements are all generally restricted by approximately 30%.* Doctors' letters refer to *an impressively scarred back of neck.*

He never did wear a neck brace. He left the carved skin open to the air, like a reminder that he should have died. If anyone was going to die in 1978, it should have been him.

There's a recent literary tradition, plausibly started by Nick Hornby in *Fever Pitch,* of using memoir to unravel a son's inhibited relationship with his English dad. The father is emotionally repressed but essentially kindly, and it turns out he was trying to express his love through action (going to football matches), not words ("I love you, son"). I have a sense of English dads in English memoirs declaring their unspoken love through pottery, ornithology, hill-walking.

This is not the story told in my fiction. I can't recommend the role of Dad in a novel by Richard Beard. My dads are overworked and distracted, arrested or beaten in fistfights, slain in battle or alcoholics who die after falling drunk from ladders. What a poor collection of dads I have assembled, of poor dads. My real dad was absent from school life but also felt missing when we were home. He turned up like a visitor in the evenings, just as we were visitors in the holidays. And then was often back out again for snooker. The only occasion we saw him for longer than a weekend (which didn't include his Saturday morning at the office) was two weeks every summer, and in 1978 for the holidays in Cornwall he wasn't a healthy man.

I can't blame a man with cancer. Can I? All these years I may have held him responsible in secret, an accusation as silent as our memories of the day itself. I don't know, so I take a second look at his pocket work-diaries. I'd found a stack of them in his study, and at first put them aside because they weren't journals — I wanted his thoughts and feelings, but had found his appointments.

Look again, I think. His yearly diaries from the early seventies through to his death in 2011 are business-to-business freebies bound in dark blue or black fake leather, about the size of a thin smartphone, perfect for the inside jacket pocket. 1978 is a gift from the Brickhouse Dudley Group, makers of cast-iron pipes and drainage products. Keep looking.

In July 1978, with no idea of what lies ahead in August, he makes a trip to Lyons to discuss French-manufactured doors and windows. Otherwise his life is active with regular commitments. He drinks and plays pub skittles on a Monday, has committees to remember, places to go (Wantage, Clifton), and people to see (Saker, Soulsby). On the first Wednesday of the month he meets staff at 3.45, and on the second Wednesday he meets with the Directors.

The month-to-a-page diary answers the question of Dad's whereabouts. A line is drawn in pencil down the left-hand side of the page from 5th August until the 17th.

While his family are on holiday in Cornwall with his wife's parents he has a full schedule of meetings, with McHugh and Eyles, and reminders of GK and the CHELT JOB. He has his Directors' meeting scheduled for Wednesday the 16th, so he can't have arrived in Port Isaac earlier than that evening, though the arrow down the side of the page denoting holiday dates changes from pencil to pen on the 17th, suggesting 17th August as the day of arrival.

Another arrow, from 9th to 17th August, is labeled BOYS TO HAKES. Did I go to the Hakes'? I can't remember. With Tim, I did go at least two years running to a weeklong Christian summer camp organized by a teacher at the school. Maybe Guy's parents drove the three of us down there. In my dead dad's study I search through his correspondence and yes, dated 31st January 1978, a letter from the teacher: *I wondered whether Timothy and Richard would be able to come down to Swanage in the summer holidays.* In August 1978, before traveling to Cornwall, we played in the docile seas off Dorset and heard about Jesus.

According to the diary, we arrived in Cornwall—Tim, Tim's friend Guy, Dad, me—the day before the drowning, on the 17th. 18th August was our first day as a recomposed group, including my dad's parents, so we did something special to celebrate the reunion: we drove to the spectacular secret beach at Tregardock.

Mum had already spent ten days in Cornwall, to see if she could cope alone with the little boys. She could. She had managed without us, and without my dad. This is not the happy family holiday I'd imagined; I had assumed we'd been together for at least a week (Nicky died on a Friday) and that our holiday had been cut short about halfway through the usual fortnight. In fact the holiday for me and Tim and my dad had hardly started.

If we arrived late on the 17th, after a long drive south, the disaster happened within twenty-four hours. My brain scrambles to make sense of this information, to find whatever logic will settle it down. If Dad had stayed away, Mum would have taken more care. She'd taken care of the little boys without his help for a week and a half, and they were both still alive. Dad arrived late. He brought the big boys with him, and to make our first full day a family treat he took everyone to Tregardock Beach.

Another observation, now that we're back at the beach: he did not dive into the Atlantic to save his son.

In old photos I use the magnifying glass to gauge how much of Dad's neck is missing. 1968, not a problem. In slides taken by my grandfather, he has a neck. I want to tell Dad to take his tie off. Ten years later he's had two operations and is steeling himself for another, and the photos are mostly of his face. He doesn't look like a man who's going to die—he looks like my dad.

I search for other clues in his letters, but those to Nicky are a scrawl, always in black ink, with sharp right-slanting diagonals steepling into loops and plunging into tails. Dad's handwriting is close to illegible, but in one undated letter from Oxford's Ratcliffe [sic] Hospital he writes to

Nicky in block capitals. He makes an effort to communicate clearly because on this occasion the message must get through — confined to a hospital bed, he has missed his third son's first day at boarding school, aged seven and a half:

MUMMY TOLD ME HOW WELL YOU WENT BACK TO PINEWOOD FOR YOUR FIRST TIME. WELL DONE! — I REALLY HAVE THREE BIG BOYS NOW.

I AM VERY WELL AFTER MY OPERATION AND THE HOSPITAL IS VERY GOOD.

He needed to write like this because an earlier letter is annotated by Nicky, who gets past a couple of individual words (*settled*, *happily*) before printing between the lines in his own no-nonsense capitals: I CAN'T READ DADDY'S WRITING.

Except after a narrow escape from death, Dad didn't make the effort. As I try to decipher his letters now, he might as well not have bothered. Only one word in four or five is legible, but he never deigned to accept that his handwriting was problematic. I wonder now whether this stubbornness is indicative of the arrogance identified for the *Sunday Times* by an exasperated District Councilor: *Most of them come from inland areas...and have no idea of the danger of the sea.*

Dad could have informed himself. In the attic I found the 1978/9 *Official Holiday Guide to Rock, Polzeath, Port*

Isaac, Wadebridge, which features a full-page black-and-white image of children hurdling gentle waves. This is the innocent fun we were aiming to emulate, so if only he'd read the contents, the guide would have been twenty-five pence well spent:

> Lifeguards are on duty on the beaches and they often see their first duty as being to save holidaymakers from themselves. You would not believe how stupid some people can be.

Like choosing to swim at a beach without lifeguards, for a start, who could have saved us from our own stupidity. If Dad had paid attention to his pocket diary, he'd have seen that 18th August was a new moon, marked with the o symbol, and new moons produce tidal bulges. The dangerous Atlantic just became seasonally more dangerous. But Dad had paid for the seaside and that was what we were going to enjoy, even if we were a family from Swindon with too much recent money who knew nothing about the natural context, setting off for our all-day beach trip to a beach that was never there all day.

I wonder now what kind of tourist chooses to take his family to Tregardock. Dad never proffered us tips for life, not explicitly, but the long hike to the special beach must have registered as a lesson that arriving at a worthwhile destination isn't easy. And that once you get there the pleasure doesn't last, due to the tide, to circumstances outside our control. The message contains a grim Protestant realism, as does a choice of school that favored 1950s shorts, elastic snake belts, and walks down the drive after breakfast.

Dad was deliberately getting us away from other people: he wanted to feel superior. Much later in his life he'd ask for a knife and fork in Burger King. At the same time, he and Mum were full of fear—between the M5 and Port Isaac we never bought layby strawberries because the Gypsies would judge us by our car and overcharge. No matter which car we happened to be in. Tregardock Beach, as a relief from these pressures, was empty of people who would judge.

The fear made Dad want to feel superior, especially to the fear, and avoiding the beaten track was a way to achieve this—on Tregardock Beach, or at a tiny private boarding school in the countryside outside Swindon. The pride, the fear, enough of both to contribute to the death of his son: at the end of one of Dad's letters to Nicky at school I eventually decipher the postscript—*I expect you are swimming like a fish now too.* Obviously not, Dad, but because you'd sent him away you had to guess, and by the time you found out the truth it was too late. Nicky was not swimming like a fish. He was floating facedown in the sea, like a plant.

I haven't finished. Don't blame the beach, Dad. Don't write a letter of "observations" to the council, because you chose Tregardock, a beach without lifeguards. You rented a house where there was no open space for energetic games, so on that vast expanse of sand we were unleashed, out of control. One more thing: I raised the alarm, and minutes earlier two small boys had been playing in the water close to the shore. Why couldn't a grown man jump straight in?

I don't understand that.

In Swindon I'm at the dining table with Mum eating steak and salad, no carbs so we can live forever. Recently Nicky has had a constructive influence on our relationship. I keep dropping by, usually to make another trawl through the study or attic. Sometimes I think I'll sit Mum down for a big definitive interview, but instead I sneak in questions here and there.

"Where was Dad on the beach in the time before Nicky died?"

"I don't know where your dad was."

There it is again — "your dad," as if since his death she can't be held responsible. I don't know how far to trust her answers. I still worry that we haven't spoken about Nicky in all these years for some very good reason. We've acted for decades as if we had something to hide.

"Never mind about Dad," I say, changing my angle of approach. Now that I've confirmed some factual parameters of the day itself, I have reference points against which I can test Mum's reliability. I'm feeling confident about how much more I know since asking that first basic question. "We have the date definitely as the eighteenth. Can you remember the day of the week?"

My brother died on Friday, 18th August 1978. Anyone can look up a day from a date, it's easy. I looked it up and the day is a Friday, another solid fact that makes Nicky and his death more real. By insisting on the details, I feel like I'm protecting his existence in the universe.

"I think it was a Saturday," Mum says. "We couldn't arrange anything over the weekend, like moving the body. That's why I think Saturday."

I don't correct her straightaway, because time and denial have a distorting effect on the past. Memories look plausible from a distance, but up close the fractures and patches become visible.

"Why did you say Nicky was bad at sport? I've read his school reports, and the condolence letters. Other people think he could do almost anything."

"I don't know," Mum says. "Maybe he wasn't good when I was watching."

"Did we actually get on, Mum? Me and Nicky. I once punched him in the face, but I don't suppose you knew about that. Do you remember any nasty rivalry between us?"

She doesn't. "You were always fighting, but boys did. You'd go off and someone would break someone else's Lego, and World War Three would break out. You were very different. I don't remember in detail, there was so much going on. You did things together, but you also did things on your own."

"Tell me about the beach," I say. I will not let go. "What are your memories of the actual day?"

On Friday, 18th August 1978 Mum was sitting on the beach checking off her children. Not enough heads, this is how Mum remembers the crucial passage of time. Not enough heads at base camp, so one of her boys must be missing and she looks for Jem, the youngest and most vulnerable. Jem is squashing sandcastles with a spade.

"Nicky wasn't there. I looked for him, but he was gone."

"That can't be right, can it, Mum?"

"Can't it?"

"You count the heads, and Nicky is missing. But I wasn't there either, because I was with him. If that's the way it happened, at least two of us were missing. Maybe Tim was as well, if he was playing with Guy Hake."

"No," she says. "Yes."

She doesn't dispute my absence from her scenario, but seems genuinely surprised. The passing of time has eroded the truth, and over the years Mum has lifted me from the water and placed me safely in her care on the beach, all of her precious boys present and correct except Nicky. She doesn't mention Dad. Wherever he was in reality, he's absent from the fiction.

Mum looks confused, as if trying to remember her reason for misremembering. What a muddle. She's lost, distressed, but while Mum doubts her memory, I'm free to question my motivation. I wonder if my harshness is to exact some kind of revenge, for the years of silence, for my cold educated heart.

In Mum's revised version Nicky wandered off, alone. He found himself in the water and was swept away. She hasn't admitted that two of her sons could have drowned at the same time, on the same day. I know this is true from being in the water, but over the years I've forgotten that in the pain and disorder so many details of the events were lost. Mum doesn't seem to realize I was involved; but then from her side she probably thought I'd remember the date. Our differing perspectives have grown apart unchecked.

"Mum, I wasn't on the beach building sandcastles." I try to sound kinder. "Can you go back a bit earlier?"

"I was packing up the lunch and Nicky said: 'Can we have one last swim?'"

Nicky says "we," not "I." In her first reconstruction Mum chose to forget I was gone, and had me sitting beside her obediently, like a good little boy. Wrong, Mum. Nicky is asking permission for us both. "Can we have one last swim?" Or maybe I asked the question. Mum's memory is unreliable.

"I was busy," she says. "I was packing up the lunch. I said: all right then, you can go. One last swim."

For the sake of a bit of social diversity, I wouldn't have chosen for Ted Childs of Port Isaac RNLI to be a retired prep-school headmaster from the south of England, but that's what he is. I'd prefer to have met the Port Isaac butcher, like the helmsman that day, Mark Provis, but Mark died from a brain tumor in his thirties. The third member of the lifeboat crew on 18th August 1978, Eddie Fletcher, newsagent and taxi driver, moved away from the village some years ago.

Ted it is. Ted Childs is a big man dressed in blue, with a round-necked navy sweater hiding half the knot of his RNLI-crested tie—a half-visible statement that binds him into the noble tradition of volunteer lifeboats. Ted and I sit side by side on a plastic upholstered bench in a corner of the operations room. To guess at his age, I make a calculation (like so many others) starting from the base of 1978. If Ted was then in his thirties—the maximum age for an active lifeboatman is forty-five—he must now be well into his seventies. In an archived photo album Chris finds a picture of the station crew in '78, or thereabouts. Ted is bald already, but the younger lads are relishing that twentieth-century moment when no one expected to see ears.

Ted has pale eyelashes and washed-out blue eyes and huge, unashamed ears. His nose is flat, honest, his lips fleshy and full. I will later have my reasons for looking at these lips more intently, but for now his appearance seems significant because he was the next person, after me, to be physically close to Nicky. He touched Nicky's skin with his bulky liver-spotted fingers.

"I remember that shout," Ted says. "Of course I do. It

was about two-thirty, early afternoon, after lunch. The maroons were fired, and at that time there was a coast-guard station at the top of the hill. The first flare went up in response to a 999 call."

The first coast-guard flare didn't always lead to the launch of the lifeboat, but Ted usually started out the door in any case. The quicker the crew reached the station, the more likely they were to make a rescue.

"The first maroon went up with a great whoosh. It was a rocket. You'd hear it and could be running by the time it exploded."

The whoosh, a raucous scattering of gulls, the bang of the maroon rocket 800 feet up in the Cornish summer sky. A shout for the lifeboat was a major Port Isaac event — first flare to summon the coast-guard team, then two more from outside the RNLI station for a full-scale launch. On an emergency call like this one the rockets would be sent up one, then two, three, with barely a gap in between.

Ted was in the street by the time the second flare banged high above the village, and the system then as now was first three crew to the station launched the boat. Ted lives a two-minute walk from the slipway; he was there in under a minute. As he and the butcher and the taxi driver zipped and buckled their immersion suits, they learned the type of incident from the operations manager — a swimmer in the water. In the language of the rescue services, Nicky was a "swimmer in the water" until proved otherwise, though according to Ted they never took too much notice in advance.

"You go," Ted says, and in those days they responded to about thirty shouts a year, "and you see what you see when you get there."

I'm not yet ready to see Nicky from the perspective of the Port Isaac lifeboat. Not yet. I look away, anywhere else but at Nicky facedown in the sea, at Ted Childs as he is today, the retired headmaster of a private prep school in Kent. Back at Ted Childs as he was in 1978, qualified to serve as lifeboat crew because he spent the long school holidays at his cottage in the heart of the village. I latch on to his hard-earned pride in a lifetime's loyalty to the RNLI, offset by the sadness of this particular day.

"It wasn't even very rough," Ted says, "and the body wasn't far out."

In his eleven years on lifeboat duty Ted Childs hauled in three dead bodies. Two of these were grown men, recovery operations. The crew knew in advance what to expect, and the bodies had been in the water for some time. With Nicky, it was different.

Go back, to the instants before his death. Nicky made so many schoolboy errors. He had a *somewhat arrogant manner*, as regretted in his school report for Summer 1977. He was *a little overconfident at present* in Maths and Art, but there was no reason his confidence should stop there: a year later he was in the Colts Cricket XI, taking unbeliev-able catches. He beat boys his age at anything, so it was no wonder his head was bigger than his boots.

The school had not worn Nicky down, not yet, and in the summer of '78 he remained *too self-assured*. One dan-ger of self-assurance was underestimating the risks of a final swim as the tide surged in. If Nicky had been less self-confident, I might have been able to discourage him. Unfortunately, in terms of his character traits, he was nota-bly assertive among older children. In the Final Order of Summer Term 1978 his age is given as 9.3 in a class with an average age, usefully provided, of 10.2. *Though the smallest in the class his agility and coordination make him always in the fore in both formal and games activities.*

If Nicky is eleven months younger than the average, there are children in his class who are eleven months older than the average; a two-year span across the class as a whole. Nicky is competing on a daily basis with eleven-year-olds, the same age as me. Nicky is *always in the fore*. He takes the lead, though the smallest in the class. He comes to believe that no feat is beyond him. He asks Mum for one last swim, even though she's packing up the camp and the tide is rushing in and everyone knows our day at the beach is almost at an end. Nicky has the idea—his idea—to leave the wide-open beach where the others can see us. We are special. We deserve the once-in-a-lifetime patch of sand behind the large rock with the best waves that no one but us has dared to test.

In *Lazarus Is Dead* I introduced an element of competition between the brothers. At the time I thought I did this for narrative reasons, because the rivalry between them created a plausible chain of cause and effect. The younger brother, Amos, wants to be first at whatever they do — first to run into the water, first to swim out deeper — but fiction isn't shaped from thin air. All novelists say this, if pressed. The subconscious must be persuaded to open.

Nick-nack paddywhack, give the dog a bone.

Fictions aren't about creating something from nothing, but something from everything: Nicky was a smaller boy in a class where other children might be two years older. He was constantly having to prove himself.

Well done, Nick-Nack, well done coming first, but keep trying.

In his letters Dad stokes Nicky's ambition, but coming first is only part of the problem. Nicky's boarding-school education puts the comfort of home out of reach. This means that in his letters Nicky is always looking backward or forward (*at half-term I hope I can find my flippers*) until his attention is permanently averted from the present (*Well dear, see you on Saturday*). Does this leave him ill-equipped to appreciate the here and now, or to identify immediate danger? It would help explain why he died.

Nicky is running into the sea ahead of me, his Snoopy pendant leaping on its chain, rebounding bright splinters of sunlight. His trunks darken as he gallops over fading waves. I may have tried to talk him back in, choosing words he'd learned how to spell—*future, sicken, stress, brink, nothing, scald*. Get a word wrong and write it out five times until it sticks: *Change, change, change, change, change*. His spelling book is full of words that at first he couldn't grasp: *scar, scar, scar, scar, scar. Rage* he manages without trouble, also *Love*.

But I can't get through to him. His head is buzzing with irrelevant nonsense, scraps from school music books, with Old King Cole was a merry old soul and *roving's been my ru-u-in*, with Birds and Their Eggs and Geoffrey Boycott's first-class batting average, and family birthdays already marked in his Letts Schoolboys' Diary for November and December 1978, beacons of a projected safe future distracting him from imminent perils as they approach.

They are here right now. He hurdles white water and throws himself at the pre-break swell of the day's big waves. We love the heave of weightlessness, the sensation of being lifted up by nature, ungrounded and free. Placed back down, ever so gently. Turn, go again.

Nicky has read *Lord of the Flies*, and together with the joy of being nine years old in the high sunshine of Cornwall, he thrills to an adventure without adults.

– *Aren't there any grown-ups at all?*

– *I don't think so.*

Without grown-ups, *this is real exploring, I bet nobody's been here before*. It's *wacco* and *wizard*, and then it is not, and suddenly *Lord of the Flies* is a novel about two boys fighting to the death on a savage unsupervised beach.

Nicky can't afford to be *windy*, because only one can be supreme and lead— *He is so confident. How different from some!* (Autumn 1977, headmaster's comments.)

Nicky is out ahead of me in the water. He is first in Geography and first equal in Scripture and also first in English, the subject closest to my heart. I don't remember him being so clever. He was stubborn, annoying, growing stronger all the time. *He has a very good vocabulary.* "Distance," "escape," "space." The evidence is there in his spelling books.

Come on, Nicky, turn around. With my hand I shield my eyes from the sun. Turn around, Nicky, show me your face and let's talk our way back with your growing stock of words, plundered from *Treasure Island* and *A Hundred Million Francs*, the story of a gang of backstreet kids in Paris. I follow him in. Being first in English isn't much help now.

Beyond the apparent confidence, and the precocious physical achievements, Mrs. Huxley long ago noted that to thrive in a difficult world Nicky would need more than a facility for mental arithmetic. *He has more difficulty in his application of the four basic processes to problems.* The problem before us is that the Atlantic Ocean is a beast and we're out of sight of the grown-ups. Nicky doesn't *understand the problem*, he doesn't *devise a plan* and is therefore unable to *carry out the plan*. By the time it comes to the fourth basic procedure, *looking back*, there is no looking back. He is drowning in the sea.

Not that he hadn't been warned: *most unpredictable—very different from the other two—shows tremendous ability but oh so careless and untidy. This must improve.*

I wanted him to be different, I remember that much. Essentially to be not as capable, and therefore less likely to carry off whatever rewards were on offer. But in truth I'm also careless and untidy, and to this day I remain unpredictable. I haven't improved as much as I should.

For Nicky, it was too late. Careless, unpredictable, overconfident, what could anyone expect? I was lucky he didn't take me with him.

I engaged my desperate crawl, found my feet, lost my footing, crawled again, struggled from the sea, accepted the useless bystander's sunglasses and ran. I ran toward the camp the family always made, for safety. On the way I threw down the sunglasses and they smashed on a rock.

After that, I don't know, but Mum does. Denial is not forgetting. The accepted scientific view is that memory is not a photograph, waiting to be discovered. Nor is it a possession that we either have or we don't. Trauma fragments memory, but I want to believe that the splinters we collect between us can be reassembled. Mum knows more than so far she has chosen to share. It's this instinct that makes me push at her defenses, and I try her out now with how the day was for me. I give her a version of the boys in the water. We were together, but Nicky found himself in trouble and

I floundered out. I sprinted back over the sand, and as I round the rocks in my distress, in my frenzy, Mum's vision of her three safe children evaporates. She gives in. I am not sitting untouched beside her on the sand.

"You ran toward us," she says. "You said: 'He's in the sea, he's in the sea, I tried to save him.'"

"I said that?"

"I remember you saying that."

We're peering at our story from a great distance, as if we weren't involved, but Mum's most obvious emotion is annoyance. A silence develops; my questions irritate her— if you're going to doubt the answer, her silence says, don't ask the question. But I don't know, Mum, I genuinely don't know the answers. Back at the camp, alive but distraught, some words must have come out of my mouth. I've no idea what they were, and until now no one else has offered to remember them on my behalf. I don't want to pounce, but given this opening I'm eager to move beyond the three safe sons and the one son missing. So, yes, I do have questions.

"Your first version was miles out. I wasn't on the beach, I was in the water with Nicky. Did you know I was in the water?"

"No," she says. "Not until now. I didn't."

"What happened next, after I came running and said I tried to save him?"

Mum offers up her next memory, if chronologically not

the next event. She is sitting on the cliff top holding Nicky's shoe. One shoe only. "I saw him floating in the water. It wasn't as rough as they said in the paper. He was quite near the rocks."

I know, Mum. Ted Childs will tell me exactly that. Trust your memory, sometimes.

"The shoe was a blue lace-up plimsoll. We've probably got it upstairs."

"No, we haven't."

If the gym shoe were in the attic I'd have found it. Often, in the middle of conversations like these, we need to take a break. Mum will read the features in the *Daily Mail*, licking her index finger before turning a page. I'll fail to get a connection on my phone, and then we're back in the room, hands free, and there's little I'm not prepared to ask.

"Did you actually see him floating?"

"Some ladies were with me at the top of the cliff. They told me he was floating."

Mrs. Kettel from Sutton Coldfield, and Mrs. Margaret Snowball from Royston. I have their condolence letters, but neither of them recounts in writing the exact events of that sad afternoon. Mum is saying she didn't see Nicky at this stage with her own eyes, or she couldn't look, or she looked and has subsequently blocked the vision of what she saw.

"Did you think he was alive, by the time you were up on the cliff with the shoe?"

"The sea wasn't as rough as they said."

"Did you think he was alive?"

"He was quite near the rocks. I thought he was alive."

Above the beach, clutching the shoe, waiting for the Port Isaac lifeboat. Someone, and Mum doesn't remember who, had been sent up the path to raise the alarm. Coast guard, please, quick as you can. At the farm old Mrs. Thom had to be in, and not out shopping or in the garden, near machines or running water, or in the coop with the chickens, or fixing the washing machine or upstairs wearing earplugs writing a thesis. Access to Mrs. Thom's landline was a potential delay, as was the physical fitness of the messenger. Delays were more likely than not.

Meanwhile, Mrs. Kettel and Mrs. Snowball offered comfort.

"I couldn't bear to look," Mum says. "They gave me reason to believe Nicky was alive."

"They would, wouldn't they?"

Everyone wants to believe that catastrophe can be averted, and I should know. I'd given Mum false hope from the moment I came running from our one last swim. Only one of us came back, and I didn't say Nicky was dead. Those weren't the words I used.

"He's in the sea," I said, "he's in the sea, I tried to save him."

Before the lifeboat arrived my grandparents led us away from the beach, up the path toward the farm and the cars. We'd have walked, I see no other solution. At my stage of life now, as I write this, I'm stronger than any of the adults at Tregardock that day, and I can't imagine carrying an eleven-year-old boy from the beach up the steps, up the path, not all the way to Mrs. Thom's farmhouse. Despite even the keenest surge of compassion, the children would have had to walk.

"Gran and Grandpa were going to drive you back to the house," Mum says. "I was on the cliff top when the helicopter arrived."

Ted Childs reconstructs 1978. Ten minutes at least for someone to run from the beach to raise the alarm, a fumble of time for Mrs. Thom to alert the coast guard, the double-rocket alert bursting above the village, then a further twenty minutes as helicopter and lifeboat race to the scene. The helicopter scrambles from RAF Chivenor, about forty-five miles away. The lifeboat from Port Isaac gets there first.

His memories remain fresh.

"On that day at Tregardock," Ted says, "we arrived to four or five people standing on an outcrop of rock, waving towels at us and pointing at a spot in the water."

No, not yet, Ted. He can bring the lifeboat right up alongside, as close as the old D-class can go, but only when I'm ready. "How long did you say the trip would take?"

"About twenty minutes. That's between the flares going up in Port Isaac and the boat arriving at Tregardock."

Add the minute I need to run from the water to my mum, then five at least before someone is sent up the hill, and by the time Ted Childs and the lifeboat bump into view, they're forty minutes too late. He didn't know that, of course. As the boat slides in, he's hanging over the side looking for a "swimmer in the water" or "a bather in difficulty." At worst, Ted will be first to spot "a casualty," so forty minutes after I left Nicky drowning in the sea he is officially a bather to be rescued, and the RNLI cannot stress this enough. The RNLI has no authority to speak of bodies or to declare anyone dead. Only a registered doctor can do that.

"The sea conditions were good," Ted says. "There was no question of us losing our lives that day. If we'd lifted him out and handed him to the parents you wouldn't even have remembered it."

But we do remember it, alas, which explains why I'm here. Only we don't remember it well enough. That's how Ted Childs can help. Ted spotted the "bather in difficulty," and now I can't put him off any longer. I've been aiming at this moment since I first went to the churchyard, whether I knew it or not, and I'm not going to back out now.

I ask Ted to remember the details. All the detail he has, for me.

"The lifeboat comes off the power," he says, "as per standard procedure. We don't want to clatter into potential rescuers who might be in the water."

No potential rescuers are in the water, not one. The helmsman Mark Provis maneuvers the boat toward the "swimmer," takes the boat round and upwind, to shelter the casualty in the lee of the hull. Though by now none of the lifeboat crew, whatever the training manual says, can pretend they're dealing with a live bather. On an afternoon of August sunshine, with a calm sea and perfect visibility, this is a lift of a body. The tragedy is clear for all to see—worse even than a body, a small drowned child.

"He was at the further end of the beach, about twenty-five yards out and it was high water. There was no breaking sea."

The beach had disappeared, and Ted Childs pulled Nicky out of seawater rolling uninterrupted onto hard black rocks. I press Ted to be as specific as he can. Dry-eyed in the Port Isaac RNLI office I feel ruthless, rational. My default attitude is emotionless and cold, a state both familiar to me and effective, one I adopt as if I'd never otherwise make any progress.

Years ago, when I smashed those sunglasses belonging to a useless stranger, I felt detached from the experience. I was looking down on the scene, and that's instinctively where I preferred to be. I'm outside the experience again now, in recognizable territory. I fix Ted Childs eye to eye and he's welling up, but he too has the English education, with advanced proficiency as a headmaster. He won't cry, but if I get this wrong he might stop talking.

Careful now. I ease the pressure by asking how the crew

dealt with the event afterward, how they coped. "What was the mood in Port Isaac?"

"Pretty somber. I suppose we stuck to the normal routines. Later we had to make statements to the police. In those days there wasn't counseling available, but I'm not sure counseling always helps."

I'm not offering counseling. I'm after the images and impressions Ted carries in his head. I want his memory.

"What did Nicky look like in the sea?"

Ted Childs lets his gaze drift round the office, appraising certificates on the walls, photographs of the lifeboat in action, and commendations for bravery. Then his eyes are back on mine as if he must have misheard and will give me a second chance to ask a kinder question, or the same question more kindly.

"Was he facedown?"

"He was facedown, with his arms out like that." Ted flops his arms up above his head, bent at the elbows, hands limp at the wrists. "I lifted him out of the water. I actually picked him out of the water."

"Was he already dead?"

I know from Chris, the operations manager, that this is the forbidden word. But come on. You can tell me, after all this time. I'm his brother.

"If I was a gambling man—," Ted says, but he breaks off. He doesn't need to finish his conditional sentence. Surely he doesn't, because in a spirit of heartfelt compassion I will allow him to stop at that. Surely.

"Would you say he was dead?"

"Well, it looked that way."

Ted got his elbows under the white armpits of Nick-Nack Nickelpin and hauled him over the lifeboat's rounded orange sponsons. You never actually know. In RNLI training the crewmen are taught not to assume, because impressions can be deceptive. Human beings want to live. Ted Childs tried resuscitation, mouth-to-mouth, three times.

I look at Ted's lips now, and will do so again. Constantly, in fact, in all the time that is left to us. His bottom lip is plump and slightly blue. He may not be able to feel his lips, after the dentist's anesthetic.

"The helicopter arrived at about the same time as the lifeboat," he says. "The winchman was lowered down, and I hooked Nicky into the winchman's harness. We practice all the time, but this was different. My most vivid memory of that day is Nicky hanging loose against the winchman, being winched up to the helicopter."

The drilled interchange between RNLI and RAF took about five minutes, according to Ted. I used to watch *Blue Peter*, so I can hear the heavy thump of the rotor blades and see the churning white water and the emergency-orange expertise that allows civilians to hope. Even after the delays, the waiting, the facedown body in the water, the onlookers could hold hope in their hearts: a lifeboat (at last!), Nicky pulled aboard, textbook resuscitation, the famous helicopter-winch procedure as seen on TV, and then the bulb-nosed Wessex yawing north and chopping hard up the coast toward Bude. All these professionals. They know what they're doing.

"Frankly," Ted says, "it was a great relief to get him off our hands."

The silence between us stretches out. Ted felt this one especially hard, he thinks, because of his job. At his school he was in constant contact with small boys of Nicky's age and size. "Every springtime I watched them jumping into the swimming pool."

And presumably jumping out alive, time and again, like a film projected in reverse. I will not let Ted go. I stare at his lips, which last touched the lips of my brother. I want to thank him, to embrace him, to never let him go. And yet. Out of habit and defensive strategy I do not emerge from the cold.

"Was there any evidence of physical injury on the body?"

I'm greedy for the remains of Nicky's final breath on Ted's warm lips, but instead I hide behind a fact here, a fact there, one more item of information to defer the inevitable. I'm a fugitive from the emotions that matter. "Was he marked in any way?"

Ted sighs. "He was just a little boy in a pair of swimming trunks, and very wet."

One more try, as if crewman Ted Childs has more to give, though probably he doesn't. Maybe a conclusive detail he's withholding, or of which he doesn't understand the significance.

"I don't suppose rigor mortis had set in?"

I ask that question in a desperate attempt to eke out a connection with the last person to hold Nicky in his arms. Ted Childs was the last person at Tregardock to see Nicky almost alive.

"No," Ted says. "He was a floppy little body."

The Boy Is Dead

Finally.

"He's in the sea," I said (Mum says I said), "he's in the sea, I tried to save him."

I was the only witness, but I never mentioned that the situation was hopeless. Not at the beach, not at the camp, not on the long walk up to the cars. I can't be sure that's true. I definitely didn't say he was dead—what I doubt is the hopelessness, because how would I know what counted as a miracle, when I was eleven? Unexpected good news could be the way of the world, encountered in earnest for the first time. Maybe I could leave Nicky struggling, but a lifeboat, a helicopter, a hospital, and the help of responsible adults could bring him back alive.

In retrospect, considering my final vision of him in the water, no outcome but death seems possible. I may have blocked that truth immediately, in favor of a hope that was less upsetting to me and everyone else. Even then I wanted the truth not to be the truth. Mum and Dad stayed with their endangered child. They too hoped for the best, for a while.

I don't remember the helicopter. I think I should. Helicopters, ambulances, police cars, we'd summoned the vehicles of every boy's fantasy, the illustrations from an exciting book. In a way my memory is unnecessary—I can pull the relevant specifications from the RNLI archive and paste them in here to create a picture: at that time the rescue helicopter in use at RAF Chivenor was a yellow Westland Wessex XS675, a humped, bulb-nosed machine, rivets punctuating the panels of the outer steel shell. On the one hand, I can misuse that information, concentrating on detail as a way of sedating emotion. On the other, well-directed research might spark a recollection.

I don't remember a yellow helicopter, of any description. But I paste it in, adding the Wessex to the picture growing from the kernel of my memory. Gradually, I'm piecing together a single day from as long ago as 1978, when I was as alive and conscious as I am now. If I can accurately re-create the day, as far as that task is possible, I'll move closer to recovering what's lost. And despite my coldness with Ted, that includes the pain I've wanted to avoid.

"Once you boys had left," Mum tells me, "your dad cut his legs scrambling on the rocks. He was trying to get as near as he could to Nicky."

Who wasn't that far out. Ted Childs said twenty-five yards, and not in open water. Twenty-five yards—twenty-two meters—but the tide is coming in and the rocks marking the cove are rapidly submerging.

Apart from this desperate clamber, Dad is conspicuously absent from everyone's memory, either at the camp as I ran in gibbering or earlier in the day. Given his cancer diagnosis, buckets and spades may not have commanded his full attention. At that time he was living with the idea of death, yet death crept up and surprised him.

His little boy Nick-Nack Pinwin facedown in the sea, 22 meters from the shore. Dad could have reached those rocks within seconds, a minute at the most, long before the runner had started up the path to Mrs. Thom's phone. Dad would have stood within swimming distance of Nicky thirty-five minutes before Ted and the lifeboat hoved into view. Ted said the body was at most 22 meters from land, so Nicky could have been even closer before the lifeboat got there. Twenty meters...eighteen, half the length of a swimming pool. The world record for long jump, in 1978, was 8.9 meters. Dad could have got halfway to Nicky in a single leap.

The other half he'd already covered by clambering along the rocks, cutting and grazing his legs. Dad, you're dying from cancer, jump! What difference will it make? Instead he looked before leaping. And looked again. Jump! But he did not jump, even though looking not leaping must have broken his heart.

He might have pulled off a stunning rescue. Or died

himself in the heroic attempt. We'd have missed him, sure, but we were already preparing for life without him. In subtle ways we'd started the work of accepting that outcome, though admittedly I have in mind an exchange in which my dad's life is traded for that of his son. Dad had cancer and couldn't bowl a decent off-break, while Nicky has *special gifts* and *always gives* 100%.

Ted Childs clipped the harness around Nicky's dead body (arms and legs through the straps, secure the lock-pin in the central lug) and the helicopter winched him up, the floppy little body hanging from the winchman in his one-piece immersion suit and dark-visored helmet.

Mum and Dad then had the walk from the beach.

"Someone told us help was waiting at the end of the lane," Mum says. "We climbed up the path as quickly as we could."

"How did that feel?"

"I don't know. I was crying. I could barely see. We chased the helicopter to Bude hospital in an ambulance."

"I'm sorry," Chris Bolton told me. "But it wouldn't have been an ambulance."

In Mum's memory the lifeboat and the helicopter, converging with an epic sense of urgency in our time of need, were joined at the lane-end by a police car and an ambulance. In retrospect she mobilizes every emergency service except the fire brigade.

"It's unlikely the police would have been there," Chris said, "and in the circumstances there wasn't any need for an ambulance." He didn't want to sound heartless, but he was an expert familiar with the procedures. "The coast guard had sent for the helicopter, so no point doubling up with an ambulance."

Chris suggested the vehicle that raced to Bude was probably the blue coast-guard Land Rover. I press Mum to remember as much detail as she can, and to forget the ambulance. She concedes the ambulance, and decides it was probably a police car.

"Or the coast-guard Land Rover?"

"Yes," she says, "that could have been it."

Mum and Dad sit facing each other on benches in the back. No sirens or lights, because the coast-guard Land Rover is not battling traffic. Of the journey, Mum remembers that Dad refused to have his legs treated. I don't know who by, now that we've erased the ambulance. Maybe by her, but he waved away the offer of support. There they sat sliding and swaying, face-to-face for the twenty-five miles to Bude, blood clotting on Dad's legs where the rocks had bashed through his skin. He is wearing his acrylic swimming trunks, at a time like this. Trunks, a short-sleeved shirt, blood on his shins and silence.

Fifty minutes later the Land Rover turns into Stratton Hospital, Bude, a kilometer inland from the coastline. "Can you see the sea, Dad?" "No." And thank God for that; it feels almost like being back in England. Everything may turn out well.

"A doctor came out to the Land Rover with the news,"

Mum says. "We were inside the vehicle when I heard the words *Dead on Arrival.*"

Something-something *dead on arrival*, the doctor said, then *dead on arrival* some other stuff. The surrounding words have not survived the proximity.

"I remember the noise I made," Mum said. "I wailed."

She remembers the wail—I see the abandon of grieving Middle Eastern mothers on the news—and then she collapsed.

The mind's camera cuts away, and the next scene is Stratton Hospital, interior. Mum is inside the building to identify the body.

"Where was Dad?"

"I don't know. I can't remember him there, except as an absence."

"You mean he didn't go in with you?"

"I might only have been alone in my mind."

What difference can it make, especially now?

"The nursing sister came out of the hospital," my mum says, tracking back. The Land Rover with Mum and Dad in the back pulls into the ambulance bay, again. "The sister gave us the news. Dead on arrival."

"Last time you said 'doctor.'"

The senior nursing sister came out of the hospital to say "dead on arrival" and Mum collapsed *inside* the Land Rover, fell to her knees on the floor of the ambulance, though maybe it was a police van. She remembers the noise she made.

"A form had to be filled in. I remember that."

The request sounds unbelievable, unbearable, but an official printed form marks the end of the beginning: the dotted lines and tickable boxes are the first dose of the documentary anesthetic to come—the death certificate, the coroner's report, the dutiful letters of acknowledgment to the many letters of condolence. The paperwork is a reminder that this has happened before and will happen again, and that the NHS has a form ready for the inevitable day when tragedy strikes. Follow the procedure. Honestly, this is something you can do.

What else is going to help? Even years later I use my various documents—the school reports and RNLI statistics—as a barrier against the great abyss. Reading and writing diverts the emotional shock, until much later reading and writing may help to bring it back.

"They wanted to know buried or cremated straight away," Mum says, "within hours of his death. The police brought us back to Port Isaac. They were very young."

Everyone remembers the police. I do, and so do Tim and Jem, because a police car meant that whatever had happened must be unforgettably serious. Back at The Mill, when Mum and Dad came back, we had a group hug in the lane beside the gate. By that time it was late afternoon, early evening. Summertime. T-shirts and shorts and plenty of light. Birds and bees. Electricity in the wires between the pylons.

"The five of you were outside," Mum says, "waiting to hear the news."

Maybe we heard tires in the lane — by the time Mum climbed out of the police car we were assembled.

"I caught Gran's eye, shook my head. That was enough."

Mum shakes her head. In the lane everyone cries. No, I can't say for sure that's true. I assume everyone cried. I invent some tears for us all. Gran goes inside to make the tea.

When I visited Bertie and Jim at The Mill I thought the space outside the gate at the back of the house seemed narrow for Mum's set-piece drama. But I make this the congested stage for that silent negative shake of the head. The family learns that Nicky is dead, and this is where and when we knew for sure.

Jem's second physical memory, after hiding behind a rock on Tregardock Beach, is of an event Mum has told him never happened. The memory remains physical nonetheless, of the type that refuses to fade.

"We were in the holiday house," Jem says. "I was woken up, led down the wooden stairs, and given a glass of sherry. It was night-time. This is a very vivid memory, even though it seems odd."

"Is that your sense of when you realized what had happened?"

I mean to say when he accepted or understood, at the age of six, that his nine-year-old brother was dead.

"Yes."

Tim is also at The Mill that afternoon, waiting for Mum and Dad to bring news from the hospital. He has no memory of leaving Tregardock, but back at the house he prays for Nicky to be safe. He prays, and he prays. Until Mum and Dad arrive to tell us otherwise, Tim keeps his hopes alive.

"Then the police car arrived with Gran inside," he says.

It can't have been Gran, though I don't correct him. I could ease off, accept the possibility of a story with two police cars. I want everybody always to be right, if these are the memories that console. Really, what difference does it make now? All of our versions exist, and for the same reason: we remember as much as we can bear.

The police car. That's when Tim recognized a terrible day for what it was, with a white-and-orange patrol car tucked in efficiently at the side of the lane, to avoid causing an obstruction. We may not remember the helicopter, but at that age we're alive to the glamour of the police. They hadn't parked up for show, because at some point I was summoned to the car: this is something I know, a reality equivalent to Jem's physical memories.

The police had established that I was the last person to see Nicky alive, and they sat me in the back of the patrol car. I remember the plastic blackness of the interior trim. Too new, too clean, I thought, as if the police car were underused, a vehicle from an alien world where no one scuffed the seats. Our Vauxhall Viva was filthy with mud and crumbs, sports equipment blocked the footwells, and prints from fidgeting shoes patterned the dash and the seat-backs. The wipe-clean hygiene of the police car was unsettling, as if the tolerances of family life no longer applied.

I'm in the police car. Now what? I've started so I want more, always more information. I go back to the well, to ask Mum, which is the purpose and comfort of mothers. Can I have some more, please? Of course you can—the mums of the world supply whatever is the opposite of the workhouse and the orphanage. Oliver Twist can ask his question without fear of reproach—can I have some more?—as long as he asks it of his mum.

"Please, Mum, tell me. Everything you remember."

Mum says: "The police wanted to talk to you, especially."

"To me?"

"Especially to you. They were very kind. They took you aside and made a point of telling you it wasn't your fault."

"You're sure about this?"

"They said it again and again. They wanted you to know you shouldn't blame yourself for Nicky drowning in the sea."

I'm eleven years old. I watch *Starsky & Hutch* on television, when I'm allowed. The police isolate witnesses when they have their suspicions.

For hours I'd feigned ignorance or, like Tim, allowed myself to hope. Unlike him, I knew at first hand that hope was unlikely to help. In fact he and the others allowed themselves a measure of optimism because the last person to see Nicky alive, namely me, hadn't cautioned them against it. I must have acted the innocent throughout that afternoon as we waited to hear dead or alive from the hospital. I imagine, as my mum stepped out of the police car, as she shook her head, that I felt some kind of relief. Finally, everyone knew as much as I did.

I can't imagine I felt free of guilt. For several years the lively N. P. Beard had been catching me up, as noted in his school reports. I punched him in the face, but failed to slow him down. I hit him because that's how frightened he made me feel, just by standing in front of me. I despised him for posing in photographs as a railway engineer. Some part of me wanted him dead. He died, and no one else was in the water but me, so no wonder the police decided to take me aside.

Two summers earlier, Nicky set up an obstacle course around the garden in Swindon. He ran and jumped for hours, competing in every track-and-field event from the 1976 Olympics, always winning gold. He was a talented athlete but only a moderate swimmer, a valiant fourth in Junior Breaststroke in the *Summer Term* 1978 school magazine.

Come face the waves, I may have said, let's see you run your way out of this one. Come on in, Nicky, if you dare.

Two brothers leave a place of safety, a camp with food and water, with travel rugs arranged by a loving mother on a flat patch of sand. All potential dangers are visible from afar in every direction, but behind some awkward rocks the older boy knows of an untouched section of beach, one that no one can see. I'd scouted the area earlier in the day, somewhere new and hidden, therefore exciting and better.

Are there any adults — any grown-ups with you?

Lord of the Flies was permanently in stock at the school bookshop. I'd read the novel too, and I'd had more years to understand it: we are a vicious species, especially the children. Only the strong will survive. Come and vault the waves, Nicky. Feel how the sea lifts us up, as if our bodies have no weight, as if we are nothing but air. Who was more likely to have taken the lead?

I didn't much like him. It's plain to see in photographs how he infuriates me, and physically I assaulted him without provocation. I didn't like him, but round a table the day after his death I hid my feelings from Dad's ambush diary.

Nicky himself was in the habit of being more honest: *Fat well you can't say that.* He tries out the unsayable, recording his awkward truths in the back of schoolbooks. Instead of smiling at the camera like a feeble conformist, he experiments: he's a bicycle mechanic, he's a welder of metal on a bridge in Wales. Nicky is whoever he wants to be. He shows off in the sea when he knows the lens is on him. He does as he pleases, and gets away with it. He is everything I want to be.

And he's nine. He is nine years old, and I'm eleven. He's catching up. The match reports in the school magazine, the *Blue and Grey*, have Nicky as a bowler while I'm a batsman, but from the pictures I see he's a batsman too. He's an all-rounder, while I bowl as terribly as Dad. In the cricket photo at the beach on 18th August Nicky is batting. I'm a fielder at square leg, but Nicky at the crease is at the center of the game—we can't get him out. He's the batsman my grandfather chooses to photograph. However I look at the image, Nicky is the one, the object of attention.

Dad feeds him easy runs, lobbing his inviting off-breaks. Nicky is a daddy's boy. In the letters he's Nicky to Mum, but to Dad he's Nick-Nack, and in earlier photos at a school sports day he's sitting at Dad's feet. Nicky is proud in the picture beside Dad and the statement Daimler. That's a serious car, but in the second half of the twentieth century the UK building trade just keeps on giving. Dad's favorite car and his favorite son, snapped for posterity.

"He was like your dad," Mum says. Did she say that? She told me Nicky was going to be a banker or a murderer. He was destined for an extraordinary life, beyond our Swindon limitations.

Up until 1978, I had been the chosen one. The last uncluttered editions of the school magazine, before Nicky pushes in, make frequent reference to the developing talents of R. J. Beard, or Beard mi. He is third in Cricket Ball, second in High Jump, first in Sprints. Three, two, one, winner. I can be the best. Every term I was desperate to feature in the magazine, and usually I'm in it. There I am by name, even if incorrectly transcribed: *Colts XV*

Rugger P. J. Beard (capt). That's me. I'm the captain already. I'm somebody.

But by *Summer* 1978 Nicky is somebody, too. He's second in Long Jump and third in High Jump and fourth in Junior Breaststroke. He has the cheek to feature in the swimming events, which I never do, though junior breaststroke won't save anyone's life. When it counts, the winner will be a savage, untaught, all-in frenzied crawl. Not that either of us yet knows this.

I'm busy looking over my shoulder, hating him for catching up because I'm one of the big boys. Eleven years of photographs, leading up to 1978, confirm that this is so. In June 1968 on a beach in Devon, at a place noted as Georgeham, I'm wearing the same dungarees and stripy T-shirt as Tim. We have no need of a younger brother and are never photographed separately, a pair of happy, fat boys gurgling with spades in hand.

In that scrapbook the village of Georgeham takes up several pages. A Premium Savings Bond is glued inside the front cover, postmarked *Georgeham 24 June 1968*, followed by Sellotaped postcards of Georgeham's church, manor, and beach alongside wine labels peeled from a bottle of Liebfraumilch and one of Riesling (*Produce of Yugoslavia*). These scrapbook fragments have a message for me. Look, look.

I do the sums, find the story: I'm seeing mementos of Nicky's conception. I turn again to the images of me and Tim in our matching dungarees and stripy toweling T-shirts.

I study the beach, the buckets, a metal spade with a wooden handle, the tipper trucks, a plastic ball. This is my last unrivaled summer, in photographs.

A year later we're on some other English beach, held back by a new baby with nine years to live. The coastline of England is where he started and where he will end, with Nicky forever little and never one of the big boys. The distinction is important, as it is in *Lord of the Flies*, where on the deserted island the boys first sort themselves out: *biguns at one end and littluns at the other*. Boys like to know their place; they feel safer that way.

At Tregardock Beach in 1978, Tim, my reliable big-boy companion, is chasing through the shallows with Guy Hake. Hake is captain of the school cricket team, of course he is, but what about me? If Tim is horsing around with Guy, then I have to play with Nicky, a *littlun*, but I know a hidden cove where the waves are fantastically huge. Come on, let me show you how brave the big boys can be.

We all remember Nicholas at the Barbecue as a bright handsome boy with a lovely sense of humor.

He was close to perfect—he didn't even tell tales, because if Mum had known about the punch, I'd have been memorably punished, and I don't remember any punishment.

Everything Nicky did he did well, be it sport, work, his music, or just kindness and good manners.

He'd been kind enough to say nothing, and now I was in his debt. He could betray my vicious jealousy at any time. He knew, and he knew I knew. Our relationship was changing.

Nicholas reads exceptionally well for his age, and has made a good beginning with all composition work.

That's *my* thing. I'd read *Lord of the Flies*, but I've never read *Treasure Island*. He was ahead of me in his reading. *He has become more sure of himself in his creative writing.* Reading *and* writing, he simply will not leave me be. He had a Snoopy pendant, and Snoopy on the roof of his kennel is a writer: *It was a dark and stormy night.* He reads widely and has the necessary imagination—he pretends he's an engineer. He's curious and tenacious. He's already judging his family on sheets of Basildon Bond. Not a banker, then, and not a murderer—Mum missed another possible option. Nicky was shaping up as a writer.

As if there aren't enough of us. I was two years and two months Nicky's senior, a gap that every year became less significant, especially when at school he was specifically commended for competing with older and bigger boys. Nicky didn't like to lose. Neither do I. I have my own school reports, with assessments of Emotional Development and more. *He is never inactive*, potentially a positive quality, though less so for a nasty piece of work who is *calculating and underhand* (Winter Term 1983). I am that kind of boy, or soon will be.

"Nicky's in the sea," I said. "I tried to save him." I have sprinted from the smaller beach, I have smashed the ridiculous sunglasses, I have not looked back.

Calculating, underhand, I did not say: "I encouraged Nicky to run into the water. I was older and it was my idea. I left him out of his depth and drowning and I didn't try to save him, not really. I was busy saving myself."

On 18th August 1978 I didn't tell anyone in the family I'd been in the sea beside him. I wouldn't tell anyone for years, until I started this book, not even my mum. I entered a locked state of denial: I blacked out my reasons for abandoning him, along with scrutiny of where that idea might have come from.

Consider Port Isaac, of all the fishing ports on the UK coastline. At the age of eleven I was familiar with the biblical story of Isaac and his sons Jacob and Esau—I'd arrived in Cornwall direct from a Christian holiday camp. In any case, this particular story was a private-school favorite, ideal filler for twice-a-day chapel, because in Jacob smoothness and brains prevail over Esau's hairy honesty. Jacob is one of us.

More relevantly to me, he stole his brother's birthright, and secured the full inheritance. Brothers are unkind to brothers. One wins, the other loses.

In Port Isaac, Nicky had it coming. My earliest memory is of my face pressed to a window watching Tim leave for school, and Tim started kindergarten just as Nicky was born. We never needed him. The big boys, once upon a time, were just the boys.

He must learn to be able to accept defeat.

I was keen to help Nicky with that particular learning curve.

He always puts maximum effort into the game.

So let's see how hard he can try.

I close in on myself, and a sharp thrill bolts through me. I am a killer. This would explain why I ration my feelings, because in the past those feelings were spiteful and the cause of mayhem. When I indulge my emotions, someone ends up dead.

The boy is dead, the grandparents are dead, the dad is dead. Memories fade.

When I last saw Guy Hake he was a thirteen-year-old superstar. His exploits in the summer term of 1978 shine across the school magazine, where he opens the bowling and has figures of six for nine in a high-season drubbing of St. Hugh's, all out for fifteen.

In Cornwall on 18th August that year Guy Hake was at Tregardock, and he later lived through whatever happened in the house. As a friend from outside the family, it's possible he didn't go into shock or close the memory down. I trace him through my mum, who knows his mum—they occasionally meet at funerals. I invite Guy round to my house, and over the decades he's aged into someone still two years older than me but who now looks younger. He has a strong-jawed, square, American face, with John Denver hair and quality specs. I'm not sure what I want from him but I ask the questions anyway, as if he may have a version of this story that falsifies my own.

Guy handles his memories of that summer with care,

turning them cautiously, not wanting to bruise or break them, often prefacing a recollection with a sensible disclaimer. "I have it in my head that..."

We all have it in our heads, but the details grow dim. That's why I asked him round. Guy remembers staying in Cornwall with us "for a time," and that he and Tim "maybe holidayed together" beforehand. I let him do the work, to gauge how far whatever is inside his head will match the facts I've assembled. He correctly places the beach in North Cornwall, the north coast, and what was odd, he says, when he remembers that time, is that unlike everyone else he wasn't really processing Nicky's death as a bereavement.

"I felt like a witness."

Over plates of bread and ham I listen to Guy's eyewitness account of the day. His memories stand up well against events I've confirmed from other sources.

"They're like snapshots," he says, "moving postcard memories. On the day, in the morning, I was messing about in the shallows with Tim. We're playing safely and one of your grandparents tells us something has happened. I don't remember exactly what was said."

Guy gets the logistics spot-on. He's playing in the dregs of waves at a safe spot on the beach while Nicky and I are farther down, to his right if he's looking out to sea. Yes, correct. He has a vision of me, once he knows something is wrong, standing down there to the right on a boulder or rock.

I have a color photograph from the Liverpool packet and can check what I looked like that day: a well-made youngster with a wet fringe split by seawater, wearing only trunks, happy to be alive and the center of a camera's attention. In Guy's head I'm standing on a rock, silhouetted against the sky by the strong August sun. I am some distance away, glistening with saltwater, desperate, beautiful, cinematic. Or so I imagine.

Guy distinctly remembers the helicopter. Finally, someone does.

He heard the distant chop of the helicopter's approach and turned to face the sea, because by then he was a way up the path. His memory is equally reliable when I test him against my recent visit to The Mill. He has the steep drive down and the hills on either side of the house. He has the bunk beds, his mind mapping onto mine and, with Jem elsewhere in the house, the four of us boys sharing a room. Then just the three of us.

"There was sobbing in the night."

Guy shuffles the postcards of his memory, but the crying and the darkness return to the top, time and again, the crying in the darkness of the night.

"How was it for you afterward," I change the subject, "when you left the house and drove away with your parents?"

"I knew not to expect any special treatment."

He means pity, or compassion. Guy had excelled at our

kind of education, where emotional muteness was a virtue. But he has, since, shared the experience at Tregardock in certain situations with others, not least when he went on holiday to Bude with his own two daughters.

"It was scary," he says. "I wanted everyone to be aware of the risks."

In his life he's had other scares, a variety of setbacks. "Traumas don't make you stronger," he says, referring to experiences of his own, "they make you more vulnerable."

I ask him, as I've asked the others who were there, what he thinks happened that day.

"Your brother was in the sea, bashed his head against a rock, fell unconscious, then later was pulled from the water."

These are not the facts of the matter. If we never agree the facts, no one can learn any lessons, to be passed on to the next generation and the next, for their own safety. Guy's two daughters will be dangerously ill-informed.

"He was knocked unconscious," Guy says, "then there was a delay before the body was found. There were big rocks there. I don't see how anyone could have helped."

I appreciate Guy Hake's effort at a general absolution from blame, which is the level of diplomacy expected from a Captain of the School. I ask him about that. His appointment as Captain over all of us was presumably a reward for good judgment and common sense at an unusually tender age. From that perspective, what did he make of Nicky's death?

"I do wonder whether you should have been playing on the rocks."

We weren't. Not that the detail matters to others, not even to the police, who told me repeatedly—but without evidence—that Nicky's death wasn't my fault. First, though, they made sure they had me on my own. Just me, in the back of a wipe-clean police car.

"It wasn't your fault. Do you understand? There's nothing you could have done. It wasn't your fault."

The drowning was bad luck, nothing more. I don't remember every detail, no one does, and by waiting so long I've lost important particulars of the story. Either that, or the piecemeal version I'm assembling now is actually full of truth, memories never distorted by multiple and changeable retellings. I don't know, I can't decide. I'm indecisive. It's one of the consequences of learning at an impressionable age from uniformed police that I'm genuinely not to blame. Nothing is my fault—I don't have to take responsibility.

Jem and Guy believe a random incident rendered Nicky powerless, either a fall or a wave, and he was subsequently washed out to sea. Mum can have Nicky wandering off by himself, happy for that luckless story to blot out any other. Her invented version is fiercely maternal—she gifts me an alibi. She swears I was on the beach beside Jem and Tim, so obviously I'm not to blame.

The day, unfortunately, has not yet ended.

That night at The Mill, terribly, we had to eat, we had to brush our teeth and flannel our faces and go to bed. Mum would never have been far away, making us younger than we were, putting us to bed as if reclaiming a time before this dreadful evening that we wished had never come. She tried to soften our newly hard lives by turning down the beds—she found Nicky's pajamas beneath his pillow.

"What did you do with them?"

"I don't remember. I'd have taken them away, what else could I have done?"

I went to sleep, or I didn't go to sleep. Guy Hake has his durable postcard memory of the sobbing in the night. I woke up, or I was already awake. I climbed out of bed and left the room, down the first section of stairs, up the other side, crossing to the landing, hoping for adult solace. I am ashamed to be looking for solace, so in the embrace of my mother's arms I say all I want is the bathroom.

I allow myself to be comforted, out of pity for my poor indestructible mum. Vividly, in all these years, I've remembered the comfort as unnecessary. Children are tougher than they look. I wanted that to be true, immediately and forever after, but I doubt it was. I just had a talent for pretending, until now.

"I understand," Mum says, "of course you can't sleep. Don't feel bad. Everything will turn out fine."

On the night Nicky died I wasn't making a simple trip

to the bathroom. I wanted to be held, and to hear the truth. Nicky was dead and I did feel bad and nothing was fine. I was a small boy and my brother had drowned in the sea, and that is truly terrible. It is a terrible and bad thing to happen, Mum, and that's okay. It's okay to say so.

3

Words Are Singularly Useless

The Day After
The Week After
The Week After That
The Rest of 1978
Forever After
Now

The Day After

On Saturday morning, the day after, Guy Hake's parents arrived at The Mill to fetch him. The strongest feelings Guy remembers are from the morning, waiting to be rescued from our family grief. He was trapped, and his disquiet started the moment he woke and came downstairs.

"Jem was up and about, and he'd drawn a picture of the beach and the helicopter. I remember how awkward that was, his child's drawing of a day out. I don't think anyone had told him to do it. It was spontaneous."

A six-year-old boy gets up early from his holiday bed to draw a picture of his bewildering yesterday at the beach. He has seen a helicopter, and in his experience of life so far his drawings are reliably the bomb. If he colors in the shapes with care, using felt-tip pens that don't go over the lines, he'll make everyone beam with joy.

"I felt passive, helpless," Guy says. "I didn't know how to react. That morning we sat around. Lots of sitting around. I didn't intervene much, apart from the Scrabble."

Guy experienced three generations of an English family coping with emotion. Mum and Dad were at a police station, probably Launceston, and facing a long, bleak day, the day after—"The police were so kind," Mum says. Jem's drawing of a happy yellow helicopter lay ignored on the table, while he wondered why no one wanted to stick it on the fridge. In the front room of The Mill we sat, waited, then children and grandparents formulated a response to a world of unreasonable sorrow. We played Scrabble.

"Really?"

"That morning your parents weren't there," Guy says. "Someone got out the Scrabble box, I suppose as an attempt at normality. We had to do something. Me, Tim, you and one of your grandparents—the four of us played Scrabble. I have in my head a nugget of sharp emotion that came out of the game. It's silly, but this is what I have."

"It's what I want. Tell me."

"In the letters on my rack I had an I, another I, an M— M for mother—and a Q. I rearranged them and said, 'Look, MIQI!' and I chuckled. I meant Miqi like Mickey Mouse. I didn't mean anything, but of all the things I could have said: 'Look, MIQI.' Tim misheard and thought I said Nicky. Nicky with an N. 'Don't,' he said."

Shut up, Guy. You have a Q, so wait for a U. Everything in its place. Don't try and be clever. Instead, Guy shouts out a word that sounds like *Nicky, Nicky, Nicky,* the already forbidden word. He didn't do it on purpose, but that's the sound, give or take an M for an N. And why not? The letters are in the bag. Try to bring him back with a single word, but it has to be the right one, correctly spelled. MIQI is meaningless. You can't put MIQI down for points.

"I was mortified," Guy says. "The whole time I was thinking what do you do? How do you behave?"

Guy Hake was a product of Pinewood School, an exemplary pupil. We shared an education and a model of how to conduct ourselves. Faced with inexpressible despair, the big boys from Pinewood sat round a table and played with words.

Later that morning, finally, after a lifetime measured out in Scrabble tiles, Guy's parents arrived.

"There was hugging," Guy says, which was acceptable because his dad was a vicar. "That was among the adults outside. I stayed inside."

Guy's dad led a prayer session that was "grounding, comforting." His father was a former army captain who had served in Palestine and now, as a commissioned officer of God, he passed on his beliefs about how the universe turned. God was responsible, if anyone was, but God was never at fault because, naturally, he was God. God was infallible, with a child's sudden death the mysterious expression of His will.

We would all of us have known what to expect from a vicar. At school in 1978, with chapel twice a day, Christian values were utterly familiar. The words of the Eucharist, as recited by Reverend Hake on 19th August, plugged us into a history older and more significant than our own. The body of Christ had been an idea two thousand years before Nicky was born, and the blood of Christ would outlast us.

My brother Tim remembers the informal communion service around the table at The Mill as "emotional." "Guy's parents didn't just come to pick him up. They wanted to be supportive."

"Were you standing up or sitting down?"

I want detail as an anchor, but I ought to know better by now: the emotion is more lasting than any specific fact, not that anyone encouraged this notion at the time. Of course not: we didn't want the pain to last, or to take root. Looking back now, the instant religion applied by Reverend Hake that Saturday feels like a clamp, an emotional tourniquet from a length of the nearest cultural material. We used a vicar because we had one handy.

When I visited Jim and Bertie at The Mill, I sat at their dining-room table until my face flushed hot—the room contained the memory of Reverend Hake's communion, and I contained the memory, and for a brief moment I and the place were one. The Saturday group communion is a definite physical memory, as Jem would call it. The event has stuck, immovable, resisting the general cover-up.

We gathered at the oval table in the dining room to praise the grace of the Lord. His ways are ineffable, but comfort is available to the quick and the dead. The Reverend Hake would have recommended that we contemplate Jesus, and His many encouraging words and deeds. I imagine this was the gist; it usually is, and may have helped us because the phrases were familiar.

In my physical memory I'm kneeling on a stone bench, and Guy's dad has taken over. He is at ease with death because he's a vicar, and he has imposed his spiritual rank. But what did we actually do?

I have the refreshed memory from my visit to Jim and Bertie. Everyone is kneeling or sitting at the table except Dad, who stands. He tells us that all his life, secretly, he has kept a journal. What he wants us to do — though I suspect now this may have been prompted by the Reverend — is to go round the table and for each of us to say a word in turn. We should share a thought about Nicky.

The day after, and already this. Lest we forget, presumably. Nothing too formal, Dad adds — whatever Nicky meant to us. He had a piece of paper ready, and a pen, and he planned to write down whatever we said as an act of preservation.

Nicky had been dead a day. He was with us twenty-four hours earlier, but Dad was worried we'd forget. Either that, or he was seizing this opportunity to cauterize the remembering, to get it over and done with as soon as possible. We had a minister at the table, so in 1978 this is probably how churchgoing people aimed at achieving closure. Write down some feelings to seal off the pain. They have to be written down, mind, or the words float free, beyond repressive control.

I'm about two-thirds of the way round the table, in the order of speakers. I have bodies close in on both sides of me, the wall behind me, the table in front. I'm paralyzed by good manners, and the habit of doing as I'm told, but I can't get out now and I'm terrified. I don't want my turn to come, but Tim has managed and so must I.

What did Tim say? I wasn't listening.

At Jim and Bertie's, with Bertie making tea in the kitchen, the room had been quiet, rays through the window and the tick of a clock. The windowsill was recessed into the thick ancient wall, like a stone bench at about knee height, and our knees would have touched because everyone was jammed in together. My memory conflated the stone windowsill and the knees, creating that physical sense of kneeling on a stone bench. The memory was false, but the emotion true: the flush can still rise, one side of my face electric, nerve endings flashing in bursts. I didn't know what to say about Nicky.

My turn. In the dining room at The Mill everyone watched and waited. "Nicky was really good at sport." I searched for a second acceptable phrase to complement the first. "He was always generous in defeat."

The words sounded passable, roughly the kind of thing I imagined people said in a situation like this. I used an intonation that suggested further satisfactory observations would follow, as in a prepared eulogy.

Instead, I burst into tears because: a) I never volunteered to speak in the first place, and b) what I came out with was a straight, barefaced lie. Nicky hated to lose. I knew it and so did everyone else. Nevertheless, that's not what I said.

Nicky was generous in defeat. The day after he drowned I tagged him as a defeated competitor, implying that someone else was therefore the winner. I didn't have to look far to see who that person might be. I'm alive, I win; but if I said by way of apology that Nicky didn't mind losing (even though he was dead) maybe he'd be generous enough to forgive me.

Just in case he was listening. I don't know what becomes of the dead.

The living either talk or they don't, and the tribute that day continued to move round the table or it didn't. I never had my full say, nor did I escape, because I was still in my seat for the holy communion. I hadn't known that was allowed outside a church, but nobody seemed to care.

We each took bread — ordinary bread from a kitchen plate — a scrap each, torn from a sliced brown loaf. Take, eat. I wasn't a confirmed Christian, but I recognized these words and most of the others from obligatory months of Sundays. Blood of Christ. I drank a sip of wine.

In this, at least, I was suddenly grown-up, though the novelty wouldn't last. The familiarity of the ritual did help, I think, and gave short-term comfort because those ancient incantations reassured us that nothing really changes. In the context of a higher spiritual reality, a dead child barely registers.

That's what we wanted to believe.

The Week After

On the Sunday we drove from Cornwall to Swindon, in separate cars. I don't know who went with whom, but we broke the journey at Exeter services for a miserable fish-and-chips. That was our usual treat on the way home. The next ordeal was the funeral.

I haven't found an order of service, and Mum says none were printed. No one had time, or the heart, because more written evidence so soon was simply too much pain to bear. Mum isn't certain when the funeral happened, but I get lucky: Hillier Funeral Service Ltd of Swindon, a family business as old as Beard's Builders, is a meticulous keeper of records. In their archived files they have an itemized invoice for Nicky's funeral—for a copy by email or post, forty years on, all I need do is ask.

The funeral is set for Thursday 24th August. Hillier's will arrange the transport of the body.

"We had no TV that week," Mum says, "no music, no games."

She remembers the silent days in Swindon waiting to bury her child, and blames the grimness on Dad. "He thought we should all grieve like him. Sit in a chair and do nothing."

Whereas in fact, Mum tells me, she had plenty to do, and having more than enough to do has since become her preferred style of life. She had to monitor the transfer of the body and choose suitable hymns. My dad's father helped with the practicalities, and as churchwarden of All Saints Liddington he advised and checked on arrangements. I see how the toing and froing kept him away from his darkroom, but anyway the prospect of developing the holiday photos would have defeated him. The canister of film brought a lump to his throat, but pictures were pictures. He selected a random address from a photo magazine and sent off the film in the post. No one knew him in Liverpool.

"We had a brilliant GP who offered us counseling," Mum says.

"I don't remember any counseling."

"Your dad refused. 'No, we don't need it,' he said. He sat in his chair."

Twice a day, from his chair, he'd have heard the dogs barking at the postman and the letters of commiseration as they slapped on the mat. *We hear that you don't want visitors or "phone calls" on your return.* Offers of help in the letters are not taken up, nor is the possibility of *a complete break at our humble home* or a bid for *the boys on their own.*

Thanks, but no thanks. We have plenty of chairs where we are. We listen to the silence, and the spring-loaded snap of the letter box, incoming, the latest flood of vellumed consolation to remind us that Nicky is dead. *Many hundreds of people and especially Swindonians will be sharing deeply your sorrow.* The people of Swindon mean well, intending to let us know we're surrounded by caring hearts that will shield us from our ugly discovery: that we're alone in the universe, exposed to terrible danger.

Those who were not at the beach that day feel drawn to speculate on the reasons why. A shock drowning flushes out the existential questions. *One wonders why these things have to happen to a dear little innocent boy.* In Swindon, in 1978, no one has the answer. *Life seems very harsh.* Yes, it does, life does seem harsh. *It is too awful*, and reading the letters once more I accept that most well-wishers are exactly as they claim: *partners in a fellowship of suffering.*

In Dostoyevsky's *Brothers Karamazov*, famously, the death of a child — any child — is offered as evidence against the benign providence of God. During the writing of the novel Dostoyevsky's three-year-old son Alyosha died of epilepsy, making the notion of divine love appear hollow. In Swindon, though, not everyone reasons like Dostoyevsky, and several letters contain sly invitations at a vulnerable time: *I belong to a small group of Christians...*

This approach to comforting the bereaved seems odd, as do others. Several letters summon the ghost of a superpowered Nicky, with *special gifts…so earnest and inquiring*. Batman, Superman, Earnest and inquiring man. I understand the urge to offer solace, but don't see how exaggeration helps—if anything, these clunky exaltations will exacerbate the sense of loss. The older generation sometimes references a harsher past: *The loss of a child is not now a common experience*, whereas once it was horribly familiar—"*other deaths, many babies*." 1978 was closer in time to World War II than I am now to 1978, but I question the value of reminding grieving parents that children have died before, and will surely die again.

Our sympathy goes also to Nicholas's brothers, who must be very sad and wretched. Oh, they are, and I'm grateful whenever a letter draws attention to the living, not the dead. *For they too must feel bewilderment and loss.* They must, they do. Bewilderment and loss sound a fair enough guess, and I use it now as a basis for how we felt. In the week after the death we are bewildered, we are lost. So much so that of the days before the funeral I have no recollection whatsoever.

"I remember the phone going," Jem says, "and Dad telling us not to answer it. The phone was in the dining room, and I remember the white door of the drinks cabinet."

So do I, now that Jem mentions it, beneath the hatch through to the kitchen, a joinered white door with a dented brass knob. Open the door, and the top shelf is packed with soda siphons. The bottom shelf is whisky and gin, Teacher's and Gordon's, and behind the spirits some bitter lemon and ginger ale—adult tastes too dry to be worth stealing, even in mouthfuls from the bottle.

For the best part of a week we sank ourselves into the house, inanimate with loss, with bewilderment. We showed few signs of life, the electricity meter barely turning, nobody answering the phone and Jem memorizing the panels on the door of the drinks cupboard. *I tried to ring but there was no reply.* Just silence in our half of a semidetached house in a moneyed Swindon street. The double bell of the telephone rings, rings, keeps ringing, then stops. Outside, up in the trees, the pigeons woo a minor-key soundtrack to English grief. Listen to the pigeons, to the sad, insistent pigeons.

With Nicky's death, the house shuts down. The stuff we usually do feels stupid, and carefree attitudes no longer apply. I can't have felt old enough for this, or wise enough. I hadn't prepared for grief, and wasn't confident any previous experience could survive it. I'd have wanted grief to teach me something, but what? People die and disasters happen—bam, suddenly and without warning, just like that. If I knew this, did it mean that I was now grown-up? Was it an essential grown-up truth that suddenness worked one way only, and anything that happened this suddenly could only be bad? And what about Nicky? I might remember nothing about him but losing him.

We spent the week in chairs, refusing life. Meanwhile, time carried on as normal, and in real time Nicky's dead body was still above ground. Where is the boy, the son, the brother? Where is Nicky now? To face the reality of death, it's important to know.

From the handwritten notes of Hillier Funeral Service I can reconstruct the movements of the corpse. The instructions to Hillier's were given by my dad's older brother, who acts quickly and efficiently, because first contact with the undertaker is made on 18.8.78, the day of death. Why wait? Do something, anything. Wrest control away from fate.

Now that I have this information, I should add that phone call to the events of 18th August, late afternoon. The day-to-forget fills up. After returning from the hospital in Bude, while I was in the police car, Dad walked the footpath into the village and at a red roadside phone box he made this call to his brother.

Despite the prompt notification of Hillier's, the process of transporting a body can't be rushed. Nicholas Paul Beard (I imagine block capitals, biro, a luggage tag round his small bloodless toe) will be picked up ("removed") from Stratton Hospital Bude on Tuesday at 2 p.m. Not Monday 21st August. Nicky's body will be otherwise occupied on the Monday.

In the meantime, the letters keep arriving. *I understand that Richard acted very bravely, which must be a great comfort to you, and thank heavens that Colin had arrived and was with you.* Did I act bravely? Who passed on this judgment as fact? No one knows what happened except me, so perhaps I suggested I was brave. If Mum and Dad were salvaging the day by making the bravery of one son a balance for the death of another, then I'm sure I'd have played along.

Nearly all the letters, even those that express dismay, reference God.

You and I know that in due time all will be explained but I must say that while waiting it all seems very mysterious.

What a perfect expression of gentle English mystification this is. Of English mysticism. Life seems very mysterious, but it's probably best to wait and see, while carrying on as stoutly as possible with 1978 — *I go to the shops most days.*

The more fervent Christian correspondents appeal *to a common faith in the life of the world to come,* and to a hope that Nicky may *continue in his new state of life to grow toward the perfection God intends for him.* Nicky is in the care of *the Great Comforter himself,* who keeps an eye on those left behind: *I have experienced how He can, longs to, and will heal such broken hearts.*

On the existence of God, I'm open to offers, and always have been. I've personally experienced a sense of divine presence on five or six occasions, mostly outside — He appears to have a fondness for the sublime outdoors, does God. He's into cliffs and white-water seas, and is transparently a fan of dramatic light, of cloudscapes and sunsets. The Atlantic coast of Cornwall is God's kind of territory, but despite the written assurances of well-wishers and friends I don't believe Nicky is a fixture in heaven, cricket bat at the ready, school cap pulled down low.

The day after Nicky died we chewed the bread and sipped the wine—God entered the story a day too late. *I feel sure you will find comfort in your Christian belief, even though at times like these one wonders if there is a God of Love.* We hoped God would be quick with the comfort, but He didn't deliver on the Saturday or Sunday, or any time in the week that followed. Sitting in chairs, nothing to do, we may have wondered what God was for.

You have three other sons who need you so. Thank God.

God takes a child but, thinking ahead, He provides three more in advance as compensation. It seems a complicated way to proceed. The most ghoulish religious apology suggests that Nicky died as a recruitment strategy, to bring the survivors closer to faith: *you can come to know the Lord so much more personally—Amazing, but true!*

But basically no, I am not consoled by the Lord. If true, a divine creator would indeed be amazing, not least because He absolves us from blame, according to the condolence letters. The death of Nicky, like everything else, is a manifestation of divine will. I have a self-serving affinity for this kind of God.

Most of the letters have a fountain-penned *answered* in Mum's writing (royal-blue washable ink), or a *Replied* from Dad (permanent black). The score is duly recorded: a 1–1 draw at letter-writing, think no more about it. Presumably the writers of unmarked letters didn't merit a response, like the infuriating Father Donald, Catholic priest at St. Savior's. How lucky Nicholas is, he writes, because dead children get *to see Him as he really is, unlike us adults, they have never encountered the world of sin and evil. Nicky is an eternal child, never will he have the problems of becoming a man!*

No *answered*, no *Replied*. Nor did he deserve any.

The Anglican vicar of St. Mary's writes in an elderly hand as wavering but determined as his Church. *The loss is so great and the distress of your other boys will be hard to bear — but at least you do not have to fear for Nicholas — he is your "safe" child now.*

Tim had spent the afternoon of 18th August praying for Nicky to be safe, and less than a week later the Church is using the exact same word, as if divinely connected. *Nicky is your safe child now.* Tim feels his prayer has been answered. Nicky his little brother is safe, which is all he'd asked of God, a tenuous consolation but one which he grasped in the absence of any other.

When I tire of the sorrow in the letters, I simply count them. Months ago, when I drove to Liddington church-yard in search of a date, I took the first step in becoming an expert: subject Nicholas Beard, dead brother. I wanted to bring as much of Nicky back as anyone ever could, which has meant retrieving the day he died, collecting the available information about what happened then and after-ward from every conceivable angle. I'd write it down, so we couldn't forget again.

So I count the letters. An astonishing 171 individuals put pen to paper to express their *deepest sympathy*, their *deep concern*, their *Christian love and feeling*. Ten people sent flowers, of which the message cards have not all perished: *Sorry to have missed you "again!" My thoughts have been with you.*

The earliest are dated 18th August, from holidaymakers on the beach, witnesses who before the day is done have already turned to writing. Most are dated between 20th and 22nd August—*please excuse the delay in writing*—and reading these letters would have been a major activity in the week of the funeral, the sympathy as pain, as a pressure to acknowledge the deficient language of grief.

I wonder why fate is so unkind to some people?

Anyone who genuinely wants the answer can do the research, as I have done. Fate is unkind because my dad had cancer and couldn't swim, and I was competitive and didn't know when to stop, and because Jim and Bertie Watson offered too low a bid for The Mill. Fate is unkind because Nicky was cocky, and because ten minutes earlier Tregardock shelved more safely and ten minutes later the beach was gone.

I don't suppose there's anything I can do.

Life is life, it is what it is, and *tragic circumstances* or a *tragic loss* or a *tragic accident* can happen to anyone. *The alternative of trying to somehow cocoon both the children and ourselves is impossible, and therefore one has to accept the risks involved.*

The risk of being alive is death. I'm grateful to the level-headed builders of Swindon, and their candid assessment of the hazards of life. We can be a pragmatic species. *I hope that both of you will have the strength to overcome this darkest passage in your lives, as life must carry on, and there are the others to think about.*

Life does carry on, and quickly: by Monday 21st August, three days after the drowning, a letter arrives about plans for a memorial at Pinewood School. The afterlife without Nicky is looking for a shape, as if grief can be organized into submission. Letters must be written and donations arranged, because staying on top of the paperwork is also a response to chaos.

In Bude, on the Monday, the duty coroner is working office hours. While in Swindon we sat our grief down, silently, surrounded by letters, the Cornwall Coroner G. H. St. L. Northey (as he signs himself on the death certificate) scrubbed up, then assessed Nicky's body. Nicky's eternal soul may or may not have transcended to a better place, but his body was on a metal table in Bude.

The coroner opened him up with a hacksaw. He pulled out Nicky's red heart and inspected it for stress. He dissected Nicky's lungs, and seawater seeped across stainless-steel, dripped to the sterilized floor. He sliced open Nicky's stomach. Northey was looking for evidence of eating before swimming, which in the Seventies almost counted as suicide.

Ted Childs said the body was unmarked. Northey pressed

Nicky's innards back inside the body cavity, then sewed up the flat stomach and narrow chest as best he could. He slotted the body with its stitched skin back into the hospital chiller.

The next day, on Tuesday, 22nd August, just before 2 p.m., a Series 3 BMW from Hillier Funeral Service in Swindon pulls up at Stratton Hospital, Bude. Hillier's has sent an extra man to help with the lifting, at a cost for the day of £22, and the two men park the BMW in an ambulance bay. They carry an empty coffin into the hospital, size 66 × 20, which in 1978 means inches. I've measured that out and it's longer but thinner than my small kitchen table. I can't read in the Hillier notes the style of the coffin, but next to the paleness of Nicky's drained flesh it will look solid and dark.

Inside the hospital mortuary the two men surely place the coffin on the floor. They remove the lid. They slide Nicky out from his refrigerated drawer. One man takes Nicky's shoulders and the other the feet. They lift Nicky up and out and into the coffin. The senior man makes sure he isn't touching the sides, out of respect, then together they screw down the lid. Stand, stretch, breathe. Screwdrivers in the pockets of pitch-black jackets. Wash hands.

Next, with an undertaker at each end of the coffin, they bend their knees, straighten their backs, lift. The coffin goes into the BMW through the back passenger door, across the seat. Not ideal, but the fuel economy on a hearse is dreadful, and no one wants to drive at 50 mph on an eleven-hour round-trip of 387 miles @ 23 pence per mile, as charged on the invoice.

Nicky spends the Tuesday afternoon on motorways seat-belted into the back of the BMW, as signed out for the day in the records. *Personal Objects?* is a reminder added by hand under **Notes** on the Hillier's memo, then crossed out. Nicky has no personal objects. He died in his swimming trunks.

From Tuesday night until Thursday, Nicky lies in storage at Hillier Funeral Service on Victoria Road. The invoice doesn't charge for visits, so I can't say whether anyone went to see him on the Wednesday. Also on Wednesday, one day before the funeral, the Holy Sacrifice of the Mass was "offered for the intentions of Nicholas Beard and family" (*JESU, by Thy broken heart, Knit ours to Thee*). I doubt any of the family went to St. Savior's to take part, not after the crassness of the message from Father Donald.

Up at the Anglican church in Liddington, the grave is being dug by Mr. Simon, or Mr. Simmonds. The name on the invoice begins with an S but is otherwise illegible. Mr. S. charged £19 to dig Nicky's grave, but Hillier's notes *Fees Not Paid*, until this reminder itself is scored through when Mr. S. (surely slow, fatalistic, with a dry sense of humor) finally received his money. He got the job done, even if no one was in a hurry to pay him.

Thursday morning, the day of the funeral, dawns onto an open grave that waits for Nicky in Liddington churchyard, the high-summer earth crumbled in a mound to one side. According to the undertaker's notes, the coffin has to be inside the church before 9.45. So a 10 a.m. start, at a guess.

"I wore a gray silk blouse and a navy-blue skirt," Mum says, fighting the black though arguably black would ultimately win. *Not blank, black*, Tim had said about everything that followed the death. "The church was full. I can't remember what hymns we chose."

Minister: Rev Powell. Hillier's knows most of the ministers; they don't need to record a first name, though the officiating priest could have been anyone. He just had to stand at the front in the collar and dare explain why children must die. Except the Reverend Powell wouldn't have known the answer, as none of us did, and as I still don't. The vicar that day would have done his best, refashioning some version of the Anglican piety that Nicky was safe. I doubt he'd have mentioned, during the service, that life is stupid and nobody understands what it's for.

"I fainted as they lowered the coffin into the ground," Mum says.

She tells me this more than once, as proof she felt strongly at the time, despite the emotional blackout we'd soon enforce. I take her word for it, because as Nicky descended in his coffin I was several roundabouts away in Swindon with my brothers and Mrs. Green, a very old lady who cleaned for my gran and of whom I have absolutely no memory.

"We didn't want to put you through a funeral," Mum says, "you were so young."

I therefore can't vouch for my own mother fainting at a freshly dug grave, nor for any other adult displays of irrepressible emotion. While feelings ran riot at the church, we sat in front-room silence with the ticking of the clock and old Mrs. Green. Perhaps she liked to knit.

"But what did we *do*, Mum? After the funeral we can't have sat around until school started. That would have been at least a couple of weeks, too long for children to sit and mope."

"Don't you remember?"

"I wouldn't ask if I did. Tell me."

"I was busy all through the week before the funeral. I washed clothes and bought food. I had to get everything ready again."

"For what?"

"After the burial we came straight to the house and picked you up. Then we drove to Cornwall."

"Sorry?"

"Immediately afterward," Mum says, "we didn't stop at the church hall for a cup of tea. We got in the car, picked you up on the way, and drove until we reached Port Isaac."

"To the same house?"

"We had it booked."

The Week After That

Tim doesn't remember, nor does Jem and neither do I. We have independently deleted the memory of an additional week in Cornwall, starting six days after Nicky died, on the Thursday, the evening of the funeral. Thursday 24th August; we're back. I can only imagine my parents were temporarily deranged.

"Did Dad think another week was a good idea?"

"He must have done. Otherwise we wouldn't have done it."

We weren't alone, again. In the week no one remembers, we shared The Mill with a woman Mum had met at riding stables, along with her two children.

"She was a single mother, this was their summer holiday. They'd been looking forward to it for ages."

"How old were her kids?"

"I don't know. Eight? Six?"

I have no idea where they slept, but that's the least of my

worries. "And these people, they knew what had happened the week before?"

"Yes."

"And they still wanted to come?"

"It was arranged. They'd have had to change their holiday plans."

Six days after Nicky drowned at Tregardock we unpacked our bags, the same bags, in the upstairs bedroom at The Mill, the same room we'd shared with Nicky. We left the buckets and spades downstairs, ready for a trip to the beach. What were they thinking of?

"Did we go back to the beach, to Tregardock?"

"We did, yes," Mum says.

"What did we do when we got there?"

"We were a family on holiday. We acted normally, as if nothing had happened."

"We must have been sad."

"I don't think we were."

"At the very same beach?"

"Yes. We didn't want you to be scared of the water."

"I *am* scared of water."

In Cornwall we attempted to pass off the extra week—the fourth week since Mum and the little boys had first arrived—as ordinary. We'd show danger and death that we were essentially unmoved. Nicky had drowned in the sea at the end of the second week of a four-week holiday, the house booked and paid for in advance. We'd had to miss nearly a quarter of our summer break for the funeral.

But Nicky was buried now, the dry earth heaped on his coffin. We might as well finish what we'd started.

The boy is dead, but what can you do? No, really, what *do* you do? We'd been sitting on the floor in Swindon staring at the drinks-cupboard door, under instructions not to answer the phone. Snap out of it! In that definingly English phrase, pull yourselves together. We could not accept, in 1978 in Swindon, the notion of legitimate emotional trauma. We didn't respect emotion as a useful human response. Pull yourself together, hunch up, shrink the target for those vast feelings as they drift close by like planets.

"And we spent a day at Tregardock, the actual beach?"

I ask twice, because even though I lived through this, I find our return to The Mill and Tregardock unbelievable. We're back on holiday, with house guests who are acquaintances of the family. We wake to another glorious day, sun shining and no special plan—say, Sunday 27th August— and someone suggests making the most of the weather with a visit to our spectacular beach. Read the tide table (on this occasion, I think, study it ever so minutely, and more than once). Come on, people, as a family. Grab your swimmers and let's have a super day out.

On Tregardock Beach, in the week after the funeral, Mum and Dad make the immense effort to act as normally as possible. I think about what this means—normal was before Nicky died. That's how to act, and it would consciously be an act, to keep the children happy. Back on the appalling beach, we three boys find some reciprocal show of our own, to keep our mum and dad as happy as they're keeping us. Everyone is performing; no one is happy. And so a disastrous template for survival takes shape.

Pick yourself up, dust yourself off, pull yourself together. Life will continue, but more harshly, and under the control of a great many imperatives: look forward and get on with it. Move on.

"Was going back a kind of running away?" I ask. "Especially from everyone who wanted to feel sorry for you?"

Mum offers a pragmatic explanation, as if psychology has no greater hold over us than feelings. "After Nicky died, we packed up the Cornwall house in a hurry. We'd left stuff down there."

Besides, we'd invited Iris Grebezs and her two children to share our holiday. In return, Iris could offer support and company to Mum because Dad was dying from cancer. For that fourth week in August, I think, a change of plan would have felt like admitting defeat.

"It gave me something to do," Mum says. "I washed the bed linen and the clothes and prepared food for the trip back down. We had a week left on the booking."

Mum heard recently that Iris Grebezs had died. The children were called Alexis and Emma, and thanks to the search-friendly "z" in Grebezs, and the fondness of popular newspapers for giving everyone's age, the *Bristol Post* helps me identify one Emma Grebezs (38) as living in Bradford on Avon in 2009. In 1978 that makes her seven, and she may have a better memory of this week in Cornwall than I do. I track her down to a marketing job in Canberra, but she doesn't answer my e-mail. Perhaps she's the wrong Emma Grebezs, who hasn't a clue what I'm talking about.

Of those of us alive and available, only Mum remembers the extra week, and she must have realized the profound oddness of going back so soon. In one of the condolence letters to my gran, the return trip to Port Isaac is all the gossip: *Eileen said they were talking of going back to Cornwall to finish their holiday. Of course, they have the other boys to think of, but if they do so I think it will be very brave of them.*

This is "brave" used in the sense of tough, of toughing it out, as when my friend Dru applied for gender-reassignment surgery. Everyone told Dru how brave she was, and she hated it. "Brave" meant tough but also "not something I would do," and by extension "misguided" and probably "stupid," an action incomprehensible to any rational, healthy onlooker.

We weren't healthy, not in the last week of August 1978, we were a family sick with grief. We tried so very hard to act our way out of it. At Tregardock we played cricket to pick up the fun of our interrupted summer. Easier to stay in bat now—one fewer fielder to make run-outs and catches, but the wide-open spaces make me feel tearful, so let's try something else. Play in the waves? I don't think so.

Or maybe we could. Champions of denial, princes of theater, we acted extraordinary emotion out of existence.

For props, we had nothing more exotic than cricket and a picnic, but we were fiercely motivated. I'd have willed that week to be emotionally flat, the new normal. Make it happen.

"I found a letter," Mum says. "I wrote a letter from Port Isaac to your gran, to explain why we went back there. You should read it."

Every discovery in the attic feels like a miracle, and this letter survived with Gran's stuff that was shunted upstairs with her crockery and walking sticks. Mum has been rummaging in the attic on her own, and has come across evidence. The extra week in Cornwall is real, with documentary proof.

Dear Mother... It may have seemed a strange decision to come back here...

It does, Mum, it does. The letter shows Mum wrestling with the strangeness even in 1978, but she reasons we need a time of peace. *We would have been smothered by telephone calls, friends, letters, this way we have been able to come to terms as much as possible, in our own way.*

Our way seems to involve the ideal of a Cornish holiday cottage, so alluring at most other times, colliding with the reality of The Mill and Tregardock, places in our recent family history steeped in violent death, and therefore the opposite of peaceful. *We have been shopping in the village and have even managed to go to the Beach, Timmy went swimming, I can't tell you the agonies we went through.*

So we did go to Tregardock, and I feel sadness for Mum,

for the letter of condolence she has to write herself because no one else has come close to understanding. *I know the men miss their children dreadfully, but to have had the joy of giving birth to a child, to have shared the delights and sadnesses with them, only to have them snatched away without warning, must leave a gap, never wholly understood.*

I've been trying to understand this gap from as many perspectives as I can, but inevitably I keep coming back to my own. At the foot of the first page of the letter I appear in person: *Richard has shut the episode out of his mind, and only when forcibly...*

I hesitate before turning the page. My brother drowned less than a week ago. I don't want to be forced into anything. I turn the page.

...reminded does he break down, so a period of peace was right for him also.

For nearly a week in Swindon I'd tried to eject the episode from my mind—out, out, then slam the door. I'd braced my back against it (not that peaceful). How now could I be forcibly reminded? Break down the door, and when Mum forced her way in, I too broke down. She says so in the letter. Please, I'm trying to keep the memory away. I'm doing all I can.

Our thoughts at the moment are that Jemmy will go back to school on Monday 11th Sept and the boys will go at the end of that week. Richard will not be ready for schoolboy questioning so we will wait until the wonder has finished.

Of all Mum's letters, this is the only one I've ever read

that doesn't contain an exclamation mark. Mum is not herself. As if to prove it, she signs off *Colin and Felicity*, alleging dual responsibility even though these are her thoughts in her voice. My mum makes the letter an official missive from the institution of marriage. She has delivered the official position taken by Colin and Felicity. No further statements will be made at this time.

I doubt we visited Tregardock every day, because there's only so much *forcibly reminded* anyone can take. Once upon a time, in a period I hadn't placed until now, we made a family outing to King Arthur's Castle at Tintagel. The village of Tintagel is about seven miles north of Port Isaac, past the turn to Tregardock. This may have felt like progress of a sort, a literal moving beyond and looking ahead.

The castle at Tintagel is a dramatic ruin spread across the rugged green myth of a cliff-sided headland. Steep paths offer precarious views of a possible epic past, but in particular I was taken with the shop. I loved the postcards, one for each Knight of Arthur's Round Table, a coat of arms in a shield above the name and a brief description of that knight's qualities. I bought six, blowing my pocket money, and my collection included Galahad, famous for finding the Holy Grail. As a reward he asks to die at the time of his choosing. I treasured those cards for years— Gawain, Percival, Tristan. Any of these doomed knights would have saved a bather in difficulty, or perished in the attempt.

They'd have perished, probably, what with the weight of the armor. Arthurian knights can rescue anyone in distress but a drowner.

In the evenings, back at The Mill, if in doubt we had Scrabble. Otherwise I can say with some certainty, despite the black unremembered void of the week, that our second attempt at a happy holiday was not a total success. From the jumble in the attic I have *The Empire "Cumulative" Cricket Scoring Book*, an A4 landscape hardback with gold lettering on a red cover. Two cricket matches have been scored.

The first imaginary game has been immortalized by N. Beard, joined in the box by his counterpart from the opposition, J. Hobbs no less, presumably full of drinks-break chatter about his career as England's greatest batsman. Nicky's match is dated 3rd August 1978. Nicky has fifteen days left to live, and the synapses in his brain fizz with the boyish alchemy of an invented cricketing extravaganza: All England vs Pakistan at Old Trafford. Nicky's imagination is engaged, attuned to the joy of fiction. Pakistan bowl seventy overs, Graham Gooch anchors the home innings with a staunch if slow century, and then the keeper Alan Knott lifts the mood with his unbeaten 132.

In reply, Sadiq and Mudasser have put on five for no loss before Nicky gets bored because England aren't batting. Only two overs of the Pakistan innings are completed (a maiden for Willis). Match drawn.

The second and final game in the scorebook is dated

28th August 1978, and I'm indebted to the pedantry of cricket's obsession with records. A cricket scorebook demands various items of information, including a line for the date. 28th August is the Monday after Nicky's funeral. We are back as a family at The Mill. Over the weekend we have visited the beach, and Tintagel. By Monday morning we need to keep ourselves occupied.

In the scorebook that day Mum has done the writing, all of it: she's trying very hard here. We're sitting at the table where nine days earlier we ate the bread and drank the wine, and Mum fills in *Pinewood School vs All England*, the match to take place at Lord's.

Players are selected and their names listed in batting order in the spaces provided. For All England, Boycott bats at one (of course) and Willis will open the bowling with Botham. In the Pinewood XI, T. E. Beard opens the batting with Howell. Guy Hake, a disappointment as Captain of the School for failing to save a junior boy from drowning, is demoted to come in at five. This match is entirely a work of fiction, but Nicky doesn't feature for either team. I'm batting number ten for Pinewood, reluctantly making up the numbers.

The match never gets under way. Mum has filled in the teams, but Willis won't bowl or Boycott bat and the many boxes and columns will forever remain blank. Every page of the rest of *The Empire "Cumulative" Cricket Scoring Book* is blank.

Nice try, Mum. Tough gig. I see myself wanting to play

along with your desperate attempt to please, colluding in the date, the place, team selection. But then the effort of imagining anything else but the very recent past proves too much. We close the book. We blink back tears, look out the window, and wonder how the sun dares shine.

The Rest of 1978

The catastrophic four-week holiday finally comes to an end on 2nd September. We have ten days in Swindon before school starts again on the 12th, and at some stage in this period Mum walks to Eastcott Smith, the butcher's, and decides in the queue that chops for tea would be nice.

"Six," she says, as Eastcott or Smith waits in his blood-smeared apron, cleaver in hand. She clears her throat. "Five lamb chops, please."

The bill from Hillier Funeral Service Ltd arrives in a plain but heavy envelope.

"I was shocked," Mum says. "It came to three hundred pounds."

I check my copy of the invoice, and the total Hillier bill is £285.01. Note that one pence, the final reckoning. Mum has forgotten swaths of experience, but she's not far off the price of death in 1978, a detail sharp with indignation. She buried her son; if that wasn't enough, she had to pay for the privilege. In today's money the undertaker's bill is about £1,550 for the 193 miles' transport, the extra man, Mr. S. the gravedigger, and sundry funeral services that concluded with the orderly burial of a nine-year-old child. This includes an Anglican ceremony and the body in the ground six days after death.

In the early-September post, along with the undertaker's bill, comes a package from Liverpool—*Max Spielmann. The Specialist Photo Printer.* Mum and Dad look at the pictures of Port Isaac sailboats, then of Nicky on his last day alive, sitting on a rock hugging his knees, gazing seaward as if at the future. The packet disappears into an underused drawer or cupboard, next to random objects destined for the bin or attic.

The efforts you have to make to help the three brothers through their great grief must impose an intolerable strain on your already overstretched nerves and sorrow.

The schedule for September 1978, in my dad's pocket diary, is similar to the working months of July and October. His meetings reconvene on 4th September (10.00 JONES AVONPRINT). 12th September is marked as *Boys Back*, despite Mum's hope for some extra days of grace. 12th September is the official start of Winter Term 1978, and from that Tuesday onward boarding school can share the intolerable strain.

"This must be terrible for your parents."

Tim remembers the exact words of adults reminding him in the weeks that followed how his parents must be suffering. They were, but ten days after driving back from

Cornwall we were offered an escape from their pain. The school would know what to do. *Plato tells us that the development of character is more important than the acquisition of knowledge*, says the 1975 prospectus, and character would be formed by a sample day like this one advertised in the brochure:

7.15 Everyone rises and makes his own bed

7.45 Breakfast (cereal, eggs, bacon or fish, bread, butter and marmalade, tea)

8.05 Inspection

8.10 Surgery

8.20 A brisk run down the drive for some fresh air

8.35 Morning prayers in the Chapel

And on goes the day in sections ordered with military precision that leave few available margins for grief. From Chapel to Assembly, then eight daily lessons and five meals (Breakfast, Break, Lunch, High Tea, Supper) with an hour for compulsory rugby and more Chapel then bed and lights out by 8.15. Then morning again, and *the boys make their own beds, clean their own shoes, wait at table and really help to keep the place tidy*. All for £525 a term, not including extras like carpentry, notepaper, and fruit.

"There was some kind of announcement," Tim says, when I ask him about our first days back at school. "It was definitely referred to officially."

It. Thank God for pronouns, I think, standing in diplomatically for the noun. We'd be speechless without "it" to take the place of *death* and *drowning* and *your tragic loss.* We need "him" for *Nicky* and *Nick-Nack* and *Nickelpin.* Dead now. Not coming back, not even to school.

"Was there a service in the school chapel?"

"I can't remember. There must have been."

I visit Pinewood's former headmaster, who took over from Geoffrey "Goat" Walters in 1977 and remained the man in charge for the next twenty years. Mr. Boddington lives alone, not far from the school, surrounded in his retirement garden by the flowers of an English summer. I compliment him on the color in his borders and the plants rising higher than the fence.

"I do it myself," he says, "but I don't know what I'm doing."

He is modest, a small part of what makes him good. As a headmaster he was never a loving presence, not exactly, but he's blessed with an unlimited supply of brisk kindliness, and in 1978 he and Mrs. Boddington had concerns enough, without pupils dying in the holidays. Society was changing and their task was to haul the school out of the Fifties and into 1978, reversing the falling roster of seventy-eight pupils. Even in my time Mr. Boddington had started a significant revival of the school, at first by allowing in the civilizing influence of girls. Day children were encouraged—pupils had parents they saw every day.

Nevertheless, Mr. Boddington has a keen memory for Nicky's death. Nicky was in the same year and class as his daughter, among the first intake of girls and who herself died in her early twenties. Nicky was kind to her, and aged nine she wrote a moving letter by which to remember him: *He was one of my favorite boys in the school. We sat next to each other for the first half of term. He was very good at sports and music.*

"So we had to deal with her," Mr. Boddington says, "as well as everything else."

We sit in his English garden with a lunch of cold meats and salad. I and other savage boys were mean to Mr. Boddington's daughter, but I'd forgotten she was friends with Nicky, and Nicky with her. At that age, at that stage of my arrested development, consorting with the weak was understood as a weakness. The daughter of the new headmaster was weak by default, partly because her parents were so close. How weak of her, to have to admit to having parents; also, she was a girl. It occurs to me now that I may have disliked Nicky for his strengths. He was his own person, not easily swayed by peer pressure. As a letter of condolence might say, *the good are taken young.*

The school devised a strategy. Tim and I should make our reappearance on 13th September, the morning after the other boarders had returned the evening before.

"Your father didn't agree," Mr. Boddington says. "He wanted the least possible disruption."

Dad thought we should start on the time-tabled evening, like everyone else—be brave, tough it out. Mr. Boddington the headmaster had other ideas. At evening chapel, in our absence, he led prayers for Nicky, for us, for the family. That first night of term, without us, he went round the dormitories and sat every boy down on the edge of his bed. He told each room in turn that Nicholas Beard, Beard min, had drowned in the sea while on holiday. Nicky would not be coming back to school this term.

Mr. Boddington asked the boarders to think deeply on what Nicky had meant to them. Tomorrow, when the older Beard boys returned in the morning, they should try to carry on as normal. Act normally, as if nothing terrible had happened.

I wouldn't have wanted it any other way. Mr. Boddington's measures against grief fit with the school's defenses against more familiar types of misery, like homesickness: a brisk run after breakfast, robust sporting activity, the original Latin of the Punic Wars. Awkward emotions could be defeated.

Thankfully. I have never wanted to be unhappy, and I could not abandon myself to grief, unlike Ralph at the end of *Lord of the Flies*: *The tears began to flow and sobs shook him. He gave himself up to them now for the first time on the island; great, shuddering spasms of grief that seemed to wrench his whole body.* If I'd given up like this, like Ralph, the teachers would have offered no more help than the Navy man on Ralph's corrupted beach: *The officer, surrounded by these noises, was moved and a little embarrassed. He turned away to give them time to pull themselves together; and waited . . .*

I didn't want to cause embarrassment, and the school was a perfect accomplice in that project. Between us we colluded to pretend that nothing out of the ordinary had taken place, and at school I was soon absorbed like everyone else. I wore the uniform gray, smelled of carbolic soap, sweated semolina and jam. I acted out our rarefied idea of normal, with enthusiasm.

We weren't looking far ahead. Aged eleven, my perception of time narrowed to the busy ongoing now, and I'd deal with grief at an unspecified point in the future. I couldn't have known it would take so long to stop playing at normal, to lose my liking for the stiff upper lip and the English way.

From the night Nicky died, I wasn't grieving and wanted nothing more than the bathroom (or so I said), and within a week I'd been spared his burial because exposure to intense emotion was discouraged for boys my age. Better to stay away and ignore the upheaval. Go back to Cornwall and finish the holiday. Start a new term at school as if nothing awful had happened.

Nicky's last direct involvement in the life of the family, later that September, was when Mum and Dad drove to Launceston to hear the coroner's findings. We can't find the written report, but it did once exist because "The Cornwall Coroner" website is clear about *the duty of coroners to investigate deaths which are reported to them and which appear to be due to violence, or are unnatural, or are of sudden and of unknown cause.* This was as true in 1978 as it is today. A death at sea requires an inquest, and the website claims that *all Coroners' records in cases of death are protected by a 75 year seal.*

My hopes are raised, but the prompt and polite Coroner's Liaison Officer in Truro is unable to help: *Sadly despite an extensive search we can confirm that we are no longer in possession of this file. Although we do have files dating back to 1978, only a sample of each year has been retained and this file is not among them.*

"The coroner was very kind," Mum says, and she can quote phrases from the verdict. "Nicky hadn't eaten a heavy lunch. That was in the report. He was a well-nourished child of nine."

Mum has these judgments of the formal inquest by heart, official confirmation that she took good care of her children. Nicky was healthy, well fed, with no one making the classic 1970s mistake of allowing a child to swim after eating. She was a loving mother who'd looked after her baby, except for the fact he was dead.

The coroner records a verdict that was probably Accidental Death, but it wasn't Unlawful Killing or Misadventure—otherwise Truro would have kept the file. The case closes, and the events between one last swim and a signed death certificate have taken barely six weeks. For the last five of those, from the final week in Cornwall through starting back at school, we acted as if nothing had happened. How was that working out for us?

As a short-term solution our 1978 English prep-school idea of normal, involving buttoned-up shirts and polished sandals, seemed to be going just fine. We battened down the hatches, an island people with experience of storms at sea. Lash the sails and squat tight below decks. The winds and the rain will pass. Meanwhile, amuse yourselves as best you can.

12th September 1978, and Mr. Boddington circulated news of the tragedy round the early-evening dormitories: "You will feel sad, but try not to show it." He was speaking to a receptive audience, a group of children who had been trained from the age of eight to excel at this very pretense. They knew the routine. First, acknowledge that sadness exists. Your parents have gone home without you: it's enough to make anyone sad. Confront the sadness, as in the preface to the *Summer Term* 1978 magazine:

✝

The news that Nicholas Beard has been drowned while on holiday in Cornwall came as an enormous shock to us. We, staff and boys and girls, will miss his enthusiasm, his lively personality and his talent more than we can say. I'm sure that all readers will join us in extending our deepest sympathy to Mr. and Mrs. Beard and to the rest of the family.

Then carry on. Apart from the shocking news from Cornwall, *Summer Term* 1978 had been a tremendous success. As always, the gloss A5 pages of the *Blue and Grey* serve up an advertorial of excitements and exploits. Beard minor, second of three, and older brother of the drowned Nicholas, took part in *life-saving partnerships* for the Cricket XI. Good boy. Not to be outdone, the Colts Under-11 cricket coach has the doomed Beard — Beard min — *taking a very hard and low catch at gully: it surprised me and moreover it surprised him.* We didn't stop living that summer just because Nicky was about to die.

In the autumn, back at school only one day late, we carried on running and jumping and painting pictures and writing French composition. The magazine for that term is *Winter Term* 1978, and I'm back on show as is Tim, though Nicholas is not surprising anyone, not this term. He has taken his last blinding catch.

Time marches on, and Pinewood School's attitude to grief is best illustrated by an article published to commemorate the death of the former headmaster's wife: *Throughout this difficult term Mr. Walters has missed only one lesson, and that on the afternoon of Mrs. Walters' funeral.* Mr. Geoffrey "Goat" Walters, MA (Cantab), on the staff since 1942, missed a single thirty-minute class to bury his wife and is praised for his *devotion to duty.* An example to everyone, he picks himself up and dusts himself off. He gets on with it, as did we.

Which, from September to Christmas 1978, after a summer of sudden death, meant a part in the annual school play. R. J. Beard is cast in a stage adaptation of *The Speckled*

Band, an early Sherlock Holmes story. He will play the role of Miss Helen Stonor, tragic victim of a crime that Holmes is enlisted to solve.

I am the inside-front cover-girl for *Winter Term* 1978. What I see is a full-page black-and-white spread of a boy who has picked himself up and dusted himself off. He is eleven years old and is getting on with life in a broad-brimmed white hat attached to his delicate pointed chin with a length of taffeta. He is wearing a full-length white lace dress, white opera gloves, a pearl necklace, and a short black cape. Someone backstage, a responsible adult, has modeled a suggestion of breasts to fill out the dress.

Look closely: the decorous sidesaddle perch on the edge of the chair, the approved posture for we delicate young women from the past. What do I see? I look terrified, a confused small boy encouraged by an eccentric school to deal madly with grief. Then again, maybe I'm just acting, because in *The Speckled Band* poor Miss Stonor fears for her life: I am merely performing her emotions.

I seek out the original Conan Doyle story, as published in *The Adventures of Sherlock Holmes* (1892), and "The Adventure of the Speckled Band" is narrated by Dr. Watson, played in 1978 by my fellow survivor and older brother Tim, aged thirteen. He is pictured in the magazine's theater review wearing spats and a tailcoat, muttonchop whiskers spirit-gummed to his cheeks. Presumably, during our rehearsals in the gym, he interacted with a Helen Stonor similar to Conan Doyle's original character:

A lady dressed in black and heavily veiled, who had been sitting in the window, rose as we entered. (Helen is grieving, and noticeably ill at ease.) *"It is fear, Mr. Holmes. It is terror."* *She raised her veil as she spoke, and we could see that she was indeed in a pitiable state of agitation, her face all drawn and gray, with restless, frightened eyes, like those of some hunted animal.*

Why does Miss Helen Stonor feel compelled to call on Sherlock Holmes? Why, Dr. Watson, because her sister is dead! Her sister! The unexplained death of a sibling is an outrage that demands investigation. Holmes and Watson therefore travel to Helen's stately home, where they make a thorough investigation of the bedrooms. Helen Stonor (for it is I) describes her evening ritual: she locks her door against the dark, but hears screams in the night. Through the grounds of her stepfather's estate, cheetahs and wild baboons roam freely, like dreams of ancient fear.

It was difficult to believe that beneath her makeup Helen was a member of a very successful Rugby XV.

It's also difficult to believe that Helen made no connection with a sibling dead only two months earlier. Equally unbelievable is the idea that a healthy way to deal with grief, condoned by teachers and parents alike, involves dressing as someone else and hiding in a fictional story that mirrors recent events.

But back to life onstage, where *The Speckled Band* is into its final act. As long as the mysterious death of Helen

Stonor's sister remains unsolved, Helen's own life is at risk, threatened by forces of disorder. Under these circumstances she has no prospect of happiness or inner peace. Unless, of course, Dr. Watson and the incomparable Sherlock Holmes can unravel how and why her sister died. Sherlock Holmes has an eye for detail, and his famous deductive method. He will account for premature death and hold the chaos at bay.

As will Pinewood School. The repression was organized, collectively enforced, so how quickly could I be made to forget? Quickly, I think. Don't speak of it, or dwell on what might have been. Ignore life's broken promise from a term earlier that *there will be no problem here. He will be a great asset to the team next season.* Forget the boy who is unavailable for selection.

I inhibited my feelings, and never looked back. Now, I'm grateful for the existence of the school magazines, as a valuable window on what we actually did. As well as dressing in women's clothes, in *Winter Term* 1978 I passed Piano Grade 2, not well, but worthy of note in *Music Report.* By *Spring* 1979 I'm scoring goals and playing Bridge and preparing for additional music exams. No more cross-dressing required. The worst is over.

Alongside Nicky's letters in the attic, I found some of my own. At about this time I seem to live a serene existence of rugby matches and bland Saturday films like *Ring of Bright Water,* about a man and his otter. In the letters home I make sure to mention I'm doing well. *I cannot wait to be home.*

Before long I'm also writing stories. My published piece in the magazine of *Spring* 1979, aged twelve, is "The Diver" and, true to the title, the story is about a terrifying dive from a thirty-foot board. *My stomach hollowed, felt strangely empty, my heart came to my throat . . . I was terrified.* Nevertheless, the narrator overcomes the terror of jumping, which is also a fear of water, because many people are watching. Then he wakes up and it's all a dream. *The diving board was my mattress, the surface of the water, my bedroom floor.*

In other words, the fear is not overcome, not outside a fictional dream. I was terrified in my own bed, at night, with no way back into the water.

"I do remember the nightmares," Mr. Boddington says.

How is that possible? I was composing stories, playing hockey (*filling that difficult inside role*), losing a squash match at the Shrivenham Military College, but I was also waking up screaming in the night and needing to be calmed by an adult. Three times at least, Mr. Boddington tells me, during that first term back, I was comforted after dark in the arms of his wife.

Mrs. Boddington held me in her arms, and Mr. Boddington told me it was over—really, the worst was over now. I'd soon settle down, and I did, into the determined cultivation of my hard English heart. I was encouraged to adopt false values by good people, and later in life I'd come across Mahatma Gandhi's intense frustration with the "hardness of heart of the educated." He meant the privately educated English ruling class he'd encountered in South Africa and India—trained to subdue their emotions and rewarded with a mention in the *Empire* cumulative scoring book. We were encouraged to dismiss our feelings for ourselves, and so lost the ability to feel for others.

My next piece of Creative Writing, published in *Winter* 1979, is called "The Confessions of an Actor," in which the first-person narrator attempts a convincing performance. He is fantastically costumed, his face elaborately painted, but he keeps fluffing his lines—*I mispronounced nearly every word, an infinity of errors.* The subconscious is issuing a protest, but through so many layers of pretense that no one heard it at the time. Certainly I didn't myself.

I look for evidence of cosseting in the first term back without Nicky, of special treatment out of pity. I don't find any. In the itemized school fees, for example, postal "disbursements" are the same this term as any other. I didn't indulge in needy correspondence. Extra fruit and extra milk appear as a separate charge, but as always this means "some" fruit and "some" milk, an orange a day, and half a pint of milk in a blue Bakelite mug. In the documentary record, normal life has reimposed itself.

"There's something odd," Jem says. He's thinking back to when he was about ten or eleven—he has a memory of an impression about a memory. "I felt there were normal years, that passed as years do, month by month. But also that I'd lived a year in my life that was shorter than the others, as if the whole year was contained in a single autumn. That seemed literally true to me. Even now, I can believe that."

A death in the family accelerated Jem's growing up, a whole year of emotional life compressed into five months between August and Christmas. If we could hold out and push on into 1979 without serious damage, we might survive. Nicky had no claim on 1979.

In random letters I find evidence of pinched disquiet. Gran wants to help, but submits to the family compulsion to keep carrying on: *I don't want to go to Bournemouth one bit, but must think of Father, we are rather at odds at the moment.*

Eventually Gran's resistance to moving on will amount to a plate she has made with a photo printed on it of Nicky and Jem climbing a smooth low-level tree trunk. She hangs it on the wall above her chair, and the rest of us ignore it. We crave undramatic weeks, in which we experience no overt strong emotion. That's our definition of ordinary, or normal, not realizing we're creating a problem not a solution.

Of inexpressible grief, or emotional crisis intruding into everyday life, I find little evidence, no matter how diligently I search. In September 1978, for example, the schedule E Assessment of my Dad's tax return "shows a considerable amount of tax unpaid." Promising. The drowning of a son

makes Dad useless for the routines of financial manage-
ment, because tax is banal compared with death. But no, on
1st November 1978, two and a half months after Tregardock, he has settled with the Inspector of Taxes. He will
pay £75 by 15th December, end of story.

In his diary from October onward the school sports
matches are systematically marked, whereas earlier in the
year they aren't. These match-days will be our points of
contact from now on, a silent touchline vigil replacing the
conversations we didn't have, not at the time or since. Dad
used to watch all the matches against other schools, without fail. And usually Mum would turn up too, and bring a
cake. God knows how we'd have managed if I hadn't made
the team.

Various awkward moments are endured, as after any
death. *I am so glad that you felt you had done the right thing
by going back to the cottage*, writes the owner of The Mill
on 12th September, but then adds a reminder about the
electricity bill.

*Unfortunately I neglected to take the meter reading before
leaving*, replies my dad eight days later, revealing a brief
window in which he wasn't himself, distracted from common chores like reading the meter, or replying promptly to
his correspondence. *I must leave you to let me know a rea-
sonable charge.* Business complete, there follows a more
surprising second paragraph: *We did hear in the village that
the Mill property was being offered for sale. If this is indeed*

true either now or in the future I would be tentatively inter-
ested just to know the details.

So for a short while, Dad fantasized about owning the house we were renting when Nicky drowned. If he'd followed this through, we might have been better equipped to keep the memory of Nicky alive. Every trip south would have been a memorial, of sorts, and a challenge to the tyranny of moving on. We might have found a healthier way of dealing with grief. As it was, Dad's tentative interest faded, or Jim and Bertie got in first. We heard no more about it.

Through until Christmas 1978, Nicky does what he can to make himself a nuisance. A school bill is sent in error marked N. P. Beard for Autumn 1978: after 18th August that year Nicky had not spent £9.08 on his Matron's Account, including garters at thirty pence and a couple of haircuts at a pound each. He had no use for a pair of laces or a term's worth of sweets or toothpaste and toothbrush (£1), not in the autumn term of 1978.

On 25th September, in a letter to Harrods, Dad specifies that *we have arranged to return two pairs of trousers to Mr. Bates of your Schools Department when he visits Pinewood this term.* Never take the future for granted—Nicky's new school trousers were returned unworn.

Elsewhere, the rest of the year is not exclusively Nicky. From one of the trunks in the attic, burrowing for relics of the period, I salvaged a *Woman's Weekly* from October 1978.

Two months after the event and Mum is reading magazines, feet tucked up on the sofa, midafternoon, nice cup of tea, licking her finger to turn the pages. Had she no heart?

I would happily, in retrospect, impose a ban on trivial magazines for at least twelve months. The existence of this magazine makes me sympathetic to Victorian ideas of isolation, the better to assimilate grief. Children would be granted a leave of absence from school. No games, no TV—Dad had the mood about right, we should sit in chairs and show some respect.

Instead, Mum has her nose in *Woman's Weekly*, "Famed For Its Fiction." I flip through, and the magazine combines love stories and stitching, short-term relief from the horrors of existence at twelve pence a week. In October 1978 Mum cut out the coupon for *Exclusive Tights*, and read adverts for chunky soup in tins. She too was making her effort at normal, at whatever solace might be taken from an eighteen-piece smoked-glass tea set.

"At the time there was a pervasive attitude," Mum says. "It happened. Get on with it."

She'd have chosen weekday mornings, with Dad at work and the light at its best, to pick the stitches from the name tapes in Nicky's clothes. Most of them could be saved for Jem. The tracksuit top from the holiday, the pajamas left beneath the pillow. I tense even now at the horror of these tiny vast adjustments.

"I did break down," Mum says, "about three months later."

At last, I think, the crash had to happen. I've read the October 1978 *Woman's Weekly* cover to cover, and the minor lifestyle options are no match for a precious child dead for eternity and the nights drawing in.

"One day I stopped what I was doing," Mum says. "I can't remember what it was, and I cried for a couple of hours."

I picture her unstitching the name tapes, or maybe up in the attic, the photographs she wants to hide dropping from her suddenly useless hands. I've made her recall this crisis and I feel relieved on her behalf that once, at least, the grief flooded out. I can imagine how much that hurt at the time. "And then? How did you feel?"

"You have to take a deep breath and get on with it."

In the Final Order for Winter Term 1978, slipped inside the end-of-term reports, R. J. Beard comes eighth out of a class of eight, by a fair distance. *Richard has not had much visible success this term*, though no need to panic. *His time will come.* This remorseless optimism is like an affliction, with the stiff upper lip as its physical symptom. The school is positive about moving forward because a bracing sense of momentum can disguise or even replace any number of more troubling emotional states. Though if we'd stopped, and looked, strong feeling might have been less troublesome than feared. *He should not be too worried over his position in the form — I believe in time he will flourish.*

The teachers wanted to be kind, but weren't equipped to give any more than that. Mr. Boddington and Ted

Childs devoted their working lives to independent prep schools and, in their combined experience, Nicky was the only close-up death. A parent would die occasionally, but Nicky was unique. Mr. Boddington's only regret about the immediate aftermath is that he didn't organize a service in chapel, but by the cricket season of 1979 the memorial of choice is up and running: *A magnificent new scorebox overlooks the cricket field — a kind gift from members and friends of the Beard family in memory of Nicholas, and we are very grateful to all who contributed to it.*

The grief has been isolated from the event and secured in a box, closed up at night and in winter, destined to weather in a Berkshire field. With the grief enclosed supposedly once and for all, my time to flourish did arrive, just as the teacher had predicted. By *Spring Term* 1980 I make the opening page of the magazine, reserved for important announcements: *Richard Beard, Captain of the Blues and Captain of the School.* Nicky is nowhere to be seen.

Forever After

I am tough and stupid, as Nicky observed in writing, the perfect combination of qualities to make repression stick. We deny, and we forget, and we stumble unfeeling through *this great testing*. Mr. Boddington places Dad's final cancer operation around Easter 1979, because it coincides with a schools Rugby Sevens tournament. As our team leaves the field he delivers me the news that the surgery has been successful. This will be the last of the traumas, or nearly.

We managed the first Christmas without Nicky, then the first birthday on 23rd March 1979. We skipped the first summer holiday—that's the general consensus, and I check Dad's diaries in which there's no indication of holiday time taken. I went back with Tim to the Christian summer camp, safe in the arms of Jesus. It wasn't the same, and from 1980 we resumed taking family holidays like everyone else, with color photos to record the fun. Me and Tim fully clothed on a beige Irish beach, slouching along with hands in pockets. Very much smaller, on his own,

Jem. Some of these holidays were beside the sea; none were in Cornwall.

The tracksuit top that Nicky was wearing at Tregardock, with white stripes down the arms and the *GO* patch on the breast, I found early on in the attic. Inside the neck, the name tape says *J. I. Beard*.

"Most of the clothes were passed on to Jem when he was big enough," Mum says. "The attitude was: it happened, get on with it."

"I know. You already said that."

The clothes and hats and the cricket bat are swallowed into family life, losing their unique personal significance. I tell Jem about Nicky's tracksuit top. "It has your name tape in it."

The two of us are taking time out from a summer day, sitting on a bench with a view of green fields. He leans forward and pinches his eyes shut, index finger and thumb blocking the light. He massages his eyeballs, working over this idea of the hand-me-down clothes. Jem was a small boy who didn't shoot up until his teens, and Nicky's clothes would have fit him until he was eleven, twelve. He lived for years with Nicky on his back.

"That seems desperately sad," Jem says. "Fuck." He catches my Tourette's, an infection passed by strong emotion from one carrier to another in the family. "Fuck."

He'd forgotten about the clothes, or never knew, but he sees Nicky's tracksuit top from the perspective of the parent he now is. The passing-down and doubling-up *is* desperately sad. He's right.

"Every time they looked at me," he says, "they must have seen him."

"They could have bought a new top."

Jem sits up from the sadness, and we agree that any of the explanations are brutal. Mum must have recognized the tracksuit with its distinctive green patch saying *GO*. Nicky was wearing it at Tregardock: he unzipped it and dropped it at the camp before our one last swim, but Mum consciously changed the name tape and passed on the top as soon as Jem was big enough. She wanted Nicky alive again. That's sad. Then she watched Jem in Nicky's tracksuit top, carefully, perhaps too carefully, safely through nine years old and beyond.

Another explanation, equally sad: Mum recognized the top but didn't think the connection with Nicky important.

Or least likely of all, since the tracksuit surfaced in the attic so many years later, she never recognized Nicky's top for what it was, and sewed on Jem's name tape unthinkingly. Jem and I mull over the long years of silence, of never asking questions like these.

"We weren't supposed to talk about what happened," Jem says, "or find out anything about it. It was too complicated."

I'm always relieved when someone else's memory corresponds with mine, and Jem agrees that the photo of Nicky on the piano appeared suddenly, after a certain amount of time had passed. Nicky wasn't always a feature in the living room.

"Mum and Dad would have been different people," Jem says, meaning if Nicky had scrambled out of the water, as I did. I think the consequences were as severe for Jem as anyone. He was left with an emptiness ahead of him, a daunting void between his six-year-old self and his big-boy brothers. Also, he left home for school after Nicky's death and not before. He would come to have strong feelings against boarding school—the conformity, the entrenched injustices—that as a family we chose to ignore. It was because he was physically small, we thought. We refused to believe he needed his home and family, because we'd blocked out those needs in ourselves.

We didn't remember, and we didn't talk. Sometimes the pressure had to be released in nonverbal ways, and as a teenager I was sent away from school: behaving badly had replaced nightmares as my unheard cry for help. On the morning of my great disgrace, Dad came to pick me up in the new Jag, and I made the walk of shame to the car. He didn't say anything, not a word, out of the school, onto the main road, halfway back to Swindon.

"We'll say no more about it," he eventually said.

We made it home in silence, saying no more about it. And then we never said anything about it, ever.

Jem says: "It sounds cowardly not to ask your own dad about your own brother's death."

"I know."

"We never got past not being able to ask."

After 1978 Dad steadfastly avoided the subject, which made it okay for us to avoid it, too. He became distant, absent, a champion of hard-core English repression, a talent that Nicky's death allowed him to explore to the full: one week after Nicky drowned he led us back to The Mill in Port Isaac. Not a problem. We'll deal with the feelings some other time.

Holed up in Dad's study, I search through his files and letters for a hidden inner life. I'm looking for the pain he never expressed, but I can't find much of a tortured soul in the bills from LIMMEX, HOME OF HARDWARE. I pick through his credit-card statements like a jealous lover — pubs, car repairs, bookshops, huge bills for medical insurance. I find the medical file: in 1979 the hospital consultant delivers a clean bill of health and looks forward to seeing Dad on the golf course.

With the cancer in remission, Dad makes freer use of his credit cards. He presses Nicky from his mind with bulk orders to wine merchants, his total drinks bill disguised across a range of suppliers: Justerini & Brooks, Windrush Wines, Majestic. From 1979 onwards Dad drank—and why wouldn't he? In March 1990, as an example, he spent £228.99 at Windrush Wines Ltd on half a case of sherry (six bottles, *Medium Dry Oloroso*), a case of white wine, a case of red wine, half a case of Gordon's, half a case of Bell's, and six bottles of Dry Martini. Which might appear an unexceptional stocking-up, only there's a similar order in February, with a change in the style of sherry (*Medium Dry Amontillado*) to add a spurious sense of discernment.

In his Graham Greene phase, Dad drank like Greene— J&B whisky because the paler color allows for a stronger mix that's imperceptible to others. In his Winston Churchill phase, he drank like Churchill—whisky and soda in the evening, with a slow-burning Havana cigar. I once borrowed one of Dad's many Churchill biographies, and discovered Churchill had lost a daughter. He therefore encouraged his secretary to have four children: *One for Mother, one for Father, one for Accidents and one for Increase.* Nicky was number three, for accidents. Churchill and my dad had got it right, and could therefore celebrate with uncounted nightcaps before bed, everything in the war room under control.

Drink wasn't Dad's problem, but eventually we came to call it his problem because that was the easier explanation. Through denial, like the rest of us, he attempted to erase the agony of Nicky's death. We blamed the drink, but the problem was the hole the drink was filling.

Deep into Dad's personal correspondence, between letters about golf-club membership and charitable contributions, I start to notice his letters of complaint. They begin in earnest from early 1979, to travel agents, oven manufacturers, to taxi companies and train operators, to the credit-card supplier. He expends excessive emotional energy on a seething complaint to a solicitor, and despairs that the local newspaper—the Swindon *Evening Advertiser*—is, despite its name, now outrageously delivered in the mornings.

I feel <u>very</u> strongly that...At least he felt strongly about something. He complains in writing, time and again, about his fate. He fights against an appalling world in which children die and seat reservations go unconfirmed and books arrive unordered from *Reader's Digest. I return your letter and statement and suggest that you deal with your incoming correspondence.*

As the years close over, Nicky fades. My grandfather stops insisting on his ritual family photographs on the steps beside the rockery: too much of a reminder that Nicky is missing, and can't be replaced. But the ache is there, the constant unspoken wish that we could somehow turn back the clock.

"I remember the babies coming," Jem says. "I don't know why they came."

After Nicky died we often came home from school to a newborn baby. Tim, as the oldest son, is taken into confidence by adult friends of the family: "Your parents are wonderful people." First he heard how terrible their life was, after the drowning. Now he learns how wonderful they are, because of how they're moving on.

"I must have spent a lot of time with adults," Tim says. "I don't know why they chose to talk to me, but they did."

In the attic I found a torn-out page from a spiral notebook:

BABY CLARK
Born 24 12 79
At 2.29 p.m.
By Cesarean Section

FEEDS 4 ozs x 4 hourly
S. M. A. Gold

Birth Weight 4000 grams 8.13 ozs
Leaving hospital 3900 8.7 ozs

This is how the substitute babies arrived, wrapped in statistics and a hospital blanket, and the fostering had started by the end of 1979. That's earlier than I'd have guessed.

"Someone else suggested it," Mum says. "The Church of England Children's Society. They needed foster mothers. I used to be a nurse."

However the arrangement came about, foster babies require the same attention as all babies, possibly more, and without Nicky our life began to change. Our family took on a different shape, with a new brother or sister every six weeks or so, though sometimes if they were handicapped or black they stayed for longer.

"We couldn't go out in the car because the pram wouldn't fit," Tim says.

Nowadays, Tim and I can arrive at the obvious conclusion that each foster baby was a stand-in for Nicky. At the same time, the babies in their white blankets slotted into the house as a new set of human concerns, helping us to avoid our own. A cheeky baby in a carriage-built pram provided a facsimile of a happy family starting over. Mum and Dad had a new child, we had a replacement sibling, and this time we'd try to keep an eye on where everyone was.

"The babies didn't work as a replacement," Tim says. "Not for me. The babies were in the way and the dogs were in the way."

The school holidays were short and time together as a family was precious, but when the fostering started no one kicked up a fuss or caused a scene or asked the simple questions. Of course we didn't—that would have involved an emotional response, which felt indulgent. At school we'd learned to do without.

"It wasn't our family anymore," Tim says. "I wanted it just to be the three of us." Or preferably the four of us, but Nicky's absence was the new reality to which we had to adjust.

Personally, I don't remember being troubled by the babies. They made me feel old, an old thirteen-year-old, but they didn't intrude on my imaginary adventures, my own way of learning to cope. I constructed epic daydreams from thin air and the sets of Elvis Presley movies. Teenage American girls could save me from anything.

In this distracted haze, aged fifteen, I signed my first official document, a consent form for my sister's adoption. The fostering stopped and legally we had a sister, then another sister. I was leaving home and they were so much younger, and handicapped. They were part of the family but a different story; even so, I have to believe that at some level Nicky was implicated in the decision to adopt. Mum isn't keen on this idea, but she'd lost a son. She and Dad gained two daughters, and whether we like it or not Nicky was still involved. Gone he may be, but he will always influence the way we act.

Not that we ever acknowledged his presence, or his power. We trusted that inhibition and denial would work, sort of. Neuroscientists now have kinder words for repression, and sometimes call it "motivated forgetting." Strategic memory loss, they currently believe, can declutter the mind and allow for efficient thinking, meaning we manage to get stuff done—scroll forward into 1979 and my results at school pick up. I'm in the sports teams and back on track.

Another concept that appears in studies of repressed memory is "dissociation." A trauma can splinter the mind into separate zones, in some of which the memory ceases to exist. One way to accelerate or imitate this process is to occupy a permanent zone of displacement activity. We avoided Nicky's death with multiple dissociated activities;

we stopped feeling by *doing* stuff, as an exhausting way to survive.

Mum was always getting involved in something, anything. She became a county councilor and a magistrate, she helped found a charity. A newspaper cutting from the attic—the probable date is about 1986—describes her occasional work with a group called Compassionate Friends, helping bereaved parents. I reckon I can guess the Compassionate Friends philosophy: what else would Mum have said, as she talked strangers through their grief, except that it's good to talk? The solution she offered others bore no relation to our ongoing family silence, but the counseling itself kept Mum busy.

Dad had his office and building yards five and a half days a week, we boys had O-Levels and A-levels, degrees, then jobs of our own. Our collective work ethic became a form of cowardice—we were too busy to look death in the face. We were actively not remembering, a stubborn ambition, but worth the effort because the platitudes felt true: time would heal. *I hope you and your family will be comforted with the passage of time.* Life goes on. Mum bought five lamb chops, and year after year we ate one chop each with peas and potatoes, fueled for another day. One more step is always possible.

These days Mum denies the denial. "When I'm asked how many children I have, I say six. I go through each of you by name, including Anna and Lucy. Then when I'm asked what you all do, which is the next question, I go through again, but miss out Nicky."

"So half the time you miss him out?"

"No one notices. They don't ask me what became of the other one."

"You have a lot of children, Mum, and your method for answering the question delivers a big lump of information. One child can easily get lost. You know that. You keep him in and you don't. It's a modified kind of denial, but that's what it is."

In the lounge above the fireplace, the golden-wedding anniversary carriage clock ticks and tocks. On the polished sides among the many grandchildren, Nicky's name remains unengraved, as missing as it ever was. I stare at the golden clock.

"We weren't in charge of the engraving," Mum says, and the conversation she had at the time has lodged in her head as a dialogue. "The rest of the family said, 'Nicky's not here.' Yes, I said, but he has been here."

She failed to convince the others to include his name, and tells me the story about the chops. She loves that story, maybe because it dates from the time before we started to forget. Not that Mum's sporadic efforts at remembering have always been appreciated, such as the improvised vigil with Tim and Jem on the day of Gran's funeral. They paid their respects at Nicky's grave, while I turned away in disgust.

I remind Tim of the vigil. "You and Jem and Mum in

front of Nicky's grave. You had your hands clasped together and your heads bowed, as if the day was his."

"Yes, I hated it. I got bounced into it."

This forever-after period is increasingly interrupted by funerals. Guy Hake's dad died in 2004, and at his funeral my mum was able to catch Guy for long enough to say how supported she felt during our *time of trial*. Guy was grateful, and comforted by this memory of his father the Reverend Hake as a source of strength. Certainly, my own dad wouldn't have known what to do without him.

"He never came to terms with it," Mum says now, "your dad couldn't get over Nicky dying."

She grounds this observation in the fact that between 1978 and 2011, when he died, they didn't have a conversation about Nicky. "We didn't talk about him. Not once." Mum recognizes how staggering this admission is, but I sense that alongside the wonder she feels a kind of pride. Dad never wanted to speak about Nicky, which was wrong of him, but look at the strength of the man, his stubbornness and powers of endurance!

"We never found the coroner's report," I say. "Dad may have destroyed the paperwork if he was upset by knowing the details were always available."

"Not once," my Mum says, "in all that time."

"In his office we didn't find any telling mementos," I say, "nothing that looked like his private acknowledgment that Nicky existed, and that he could make us feel."

But as scientists like to say, the absence of evidence is not evidence of absence. Perhaps I've yet to search in the relevant place. I look up 18th August in all of Dad's pocket diaries after 1978. He either has meetings or he doesn't, but I see no indication of a day of special remembrance. I check 18th August on the health charts the doctors encouraged him to keep toward the end. Nothing out of the ordinary—on 18th August 2008, the thirtieth anniversary of Nicky's death, his blood pressure is up but his pulse is at its lowest for a month. Maybe he forgot the date, like I did.

In 2011 the cancer came back. Dad would not be challenging his grandfather for Longest Working Life, but he did have Galahad's privilege, more or less, of knowing when he was going to die. He was given three months, and decided to write his life story, the confession of a dying man, the equivalent of a final phone call from Death Row. At last he had his chance, he could try to speak to us.

He made some notes on a spreadsheet, with the years and months in the left-hand column. In 1965, Feb, he has *MARRIAGE!* and in Nov of the same year, *Tim*. In 1967, Jan—*Richy*. 1969, the year of Nicky's birth, is blank. 1978 records his grandfather's 100th birthday (April) but amazingly, for Aug 1978 his mind has gone blank again—*Holiday?*

Of the writing itself, he managed half a page. A couple of lines announcing his possibly not uncommon project of settling his final account, then a line or two about finding the actual writing harder than expected.

"I am a very superficial person," he concluded. "There is nothing beneath the surface."

By the end he didn't dare look; even a glance inside was a risk too great to take. When no more steps were possible he retreated to his bed in the bungalow, along the corridor from the lounge where I would come to ask Mum my belated questions. I did broach the subject of Nicky with him before he died, because bedridden he was a captive audience and neither of us had much to lose.

"Dad, tell me about the diaries. In Cornwall, the day after Nicky died, we gathered round a table in the holiday house. You said you kept a diary that not even Mum knew about. You wanted each of us to say something about Nicky, so you could write it down."

"I don't remember."

"It was before we took communion in the holiday house."

"I never kept a diary."

"Never?"

"Oh, Richy," he said, and waggled his fingers in the air like he used to when very drunk. It was a gesture that seemed to mean all life is dust and will fly away and he didn't care, so neither should I.

"Dad, you said you kept a diary. Have you ever kept that kind of diary?"

"No."

At the very end he reached out his hand, and I didn't take it. A bit late for that, I thought, a bit late now for emotional needs. In every other respect I was sad and attentive, as demanded by the occasion, even when all he could say was "What's the time?" and, possibly, "Water." He often asked for water. His kidneys had packed up, but he felt thirsty. I fed him blots of water from the spout of a small striped teapot. His eyes went gray like a troubled sky and his lips thinned, pulled back into his mouth. His chin, too, somehow receded. He looked like his mother, then he died.

I haven't mourned him, and I did not cry at his funeral. I've read books that say trauma memories can be reawakened by an extreme emotional state that matches the original experience. If that emotion is grief, I knew when my dad died to carry on as if nothing awful had happened. A lesson he taught me himself.

Now

The dead are not always remembered. Nicky's infant school before Pinewood, Kingsbury Hill House in Marlborough, dedicated a Music Cup to his memory, and I have a headmaster's letter bursting with good intentions: *8th June 1979, Dear Mr. and Mrs. Beard, The cup which you so kindly brought in this morning glistens in my study and is such a timely reminder of how we all should turn personal tragedy and suffering into a vehicle for others' joy and happiness.*

The cup has been lost, the school itself a memory: closed in the year 2000, the land sold to developers. The school buildings have become luxury flats. We don't remember, no matter how eloquently we say we will.

I imagine something sporting, wrote Mr. Boddington from Pinewood, and in 1978 members and friends of the Beard family donated money *for some permanent memorial*. The cricket scorebox at Pinewood School lasted thirty years, and now clings to useful life as a groundsman's shed.

On a cold February day I decide to return the school magazines on loan from Mr. Field. I leave them inside the main door and walk across the frosted pitches to the battered scorebox. I have a screwdriver in my pocket, to unscrew the brass plaque from the door. No one else is remembering but me.

Then I realize the plaque exists for exactly that reason, so I stare at it for a while before leaving it be. In whatever lifetime the plaque has left, its words may still bring Nicky, or an idea of him, into someone's living mind. Nor are the facts I've gathered about Nicky's life exclusively mine. When I talk to Mum I give her a summary of Nicky's school reports and his appearances in the *Blue and Grey*, I list his certificates and show her photographs in which he's batting, swimming, running. "Why did you think he was going to be a banker, or a murderer?"

"I don't know," Mum says. "I don't know why I remembered him like I did."

Mum sounds bemused but also defiant, as if protecting the falseness of the memory. After all, why should I know any better? I show her a receipt for Nicky's place on the waiting list for the secondary school where his big-boy elder brothers went. "You told me the plan was to send him somewhere less competitive, where as a non-sportsman without too many brains he'd be better able to cope."

"I was wrong. Or your dad told me that was going to happen. I never knew he was on the list."

Mum examines the piece of paper as if the truth in black

and white is a lie she can see straight through. She fetches her glasses and reads the receipt again, and I wish she'd trust the documents as I do. This is our past as recorded in writing, evidence that travels securely through time. Mum, this is 1978 as it was.

All I did was look, and then assemble the evidence. I disagree with the many letter writers from 1978 who didn't know what to say. *There really aren't words that can express my feelings.* This was the most common reaction, but they weren't trying hard enough, or hadn't completed the training. The words exist, and techniques for effective communication can be honed with practice. The language exists to make sense of grief, I'm sure this must be true. I've searched out *words that can express my feelings.*

In midlife, denial and distraction wear thin. I could see through myself, from the present into a past of transparent strategies worthy of international acclaim: *Richard Beard (UK), Longest Unbroken Period of Denial.* And looking into the future, I could see more of the same: write about anything else but this. Then suddenly I was free to rummage through my dad's old files. It felt like the time was right.

When finally I faced the reality of a child's death—the dates, the documents, the facts—I realized this was always the story I'd been trying to write. In among the 1978 condolence letters a woman called Edna, half of a married unit called *Edna and Tom*, is terribly sad and has been thinking of little else. She wonders what on earth anyone can do:

Tom said: you don't have to write a book to say how sad and sorry you are about the loss of a little chap. But...

But, Edna, maybe you do. Maybe all these years later I did.

Nearly four decades after the event, I have carried out my version of an inquest. I've tried to stop time in Cornwall on a single day, though I've never before worked like this, surrounded by the debris of the past. I navigate a floor covered in photos and school reports, letters and random items of vintage clothing. I sit down, I stand up, I welcome and curse the return of feeling and kick my chair across the room. Feel, damn you, feel something or forget, forget it ever happened.

"One hopes it was over quickly," Mum says, thinking of Nicky in the water, because the day and the boy and the death are newly open for discussion. Their time has come again.

"He wasn't in pain," she says, a statement neither of us can substantiate. He was terrified, I know that. I saw his strained tight-lipped face. I felt the terror of death.

Mum hasn't finished: "He was doing what he wanted to do."

He was a runner, Mum, and a cricketer. He understood parabolas and bounce, the certainties of the level playing field. If you think he was a swimmer you pay too much attention to holiday snaps. Of Mum's three hopes, the speed of it is most likely to be true. Nicky probably died quickly. One swallow of seawater, Chris Bolton of the Port

Isaac RNLI told me, and panic can kill. Quickly, very quickly, the lungs fill up and Nicky surrenders, facedown, finished.

Bad luck, circumstance. Too young, too old. Too early, too late. I was immortal and he was not.

Aiming for as complete a picture as possible, I wrote to the bystanders on the beach that day, because in the formal, correct manner they'd headed their condolence letters with a return address. I reached out to the useless man on the rocks, who once wrote: *You don't remember me I am sure, however I was one of the people who clambered along the rocks with you at Tregardock last Friday afternoon in an attempt to save your son.*

His original letter traveled first class in 1978 from Sutton Coldfield, with no phone number, but anyway I couldn't have explained on the phone. *Please do not feel a need to answer this letter.* He writes to us then, I write back to him now. We think, we write. We live in 1978.

These days, no reply. I look up the address on Zoopla, and the house has been sold several times over since 1978. My envelope, for all I know, is lost among pizza leaflets and boiler discounts.

When writing fails, for more material I can visit Tregardock any time I like, because Cornwall isn't as distant as it was. Now, when I climb into the car, I presume I won't need my dad's handwritten directions, but more often than not I tend to get lost. And when I do eventually arrive at the beach, literally half the time the beach isn't there.

I rarely cry on the path, not these days. My inquest has made me reassess why I sobbed out loud on the first trip back. Nicky died here, but I was also blindly reliving the horror of the week after the funeral, back so soon with the feelings raw. Every time I come to Tregardock I revisit the death but also the refusal to grieve, the immediate repression, and I regret that epic success. I reexperience the pounds-per-square-inch pressure on an eleven-year-old in trunks; the same trunks as one week earlier.

What am I actually looking for, on these trips to the beach? The sand isn't home to hidden documents, and that's an added motivation: my search for feelings in the paperwork can keep those feelings at bay. My dry-eyed desk research can sometimes feel like emotion managed. So I like to visit Tregardock, to make the inquest complete: I'm seeking out raw feeling, of the type I've denied for so long, but how will I recognize what I'm looking for? It will probably make me cry.

From the beach, if I find the sand submerged at high tide, I walk up to the farmhouse, and from the farmhouse I retrace my steps to the beach. Then back to the farmhouse. In the wind, on the wet slate of the path, I cast about for a memory of leaving a brother behind, the first time, of walking uphill from the beach to the cars while Nicky was drifting in the water. I can't be sure of the memory, because I walked this path nine or ten or eleven days later, doing my best to forget. I try to imagine the walk to the beach in the final week, after the funeral, and I see a relay of anxious glances:

"All right?"

"Fine."

To the beach, to the farmhouse. Back to the beach, I play all the roles. Walking down, I'm eleven, a child anticipating fun. *Can you see the sea?* And a week and a bit later I'm pretending nothing has changed. *Yes, Dad, I can see the sea.* Walking up, I'm slow with brothers and grandparents, leaving Mum and Dad at the water's edge desperate with unfounded hope. I consider the lies I may have told, to others and to myself. *He's in the sea, I tried to save him.* Nicky was dead.

I walk back up in the skin of my dad, shins bleeding, then as Mum, clutching a size-three shoe and swallowing her heart. I try every permutation, searching for a combination that may open up a high-fidelity memory, or a ravishing pain, or an insight of stunning significance. An ending, a beginning, or if neither of these I seek out the safety of knowing that nothing can surprise me now. Each trip up and down is a reenactment, like a lonely weekend hobby that never captures exactly how it was on the day. At the reenactment of the Battle of Hastings, there's always a bloke in specs.

I run up as the messenger, whoever was sent to raise the alarm with Mrs. Thom at the farmhouse. At the farm, out of breath (13 minutes 27 seconds) I sometimes see Mrs.

Thom's daughter as she checks on the gates with her dog. She is the age now that Mrs. Thom was then. I say hello but not much more, though once I phoned about a room she had to let in the farmhouse. She was happy to chat.

"It's such a dangerous beach," Mrs. Thom's daughter said. "Which one was yours?"

"1978 — a small boy."

"I don't remember that one."

"I'm writing about it."

"Oh no. We have trouble enough with surfers. They block the road. Don't write an article. 'Best secret beach,' that kind of thing."

Not what I had in mind, not exactly. Recently at Tregardock I stood in the January rain on the brown sand, squinting at the spray from heavy gray breakers. The week we spent in Cornwall after the funeral, I think, acts as a barrier. I *had* been to Tregardock since Nicky died, possibly more than once, less than a fortnight later. That extra, forgotten week obstructs contact with the day itself, because the fencing was erected almost immediately. Any emotion I feel at the beach is triggered by Nicky's death, but also by the painful effort to suppress his death.

I visit the crags of Tintagel. Out of season, I'm alone on the steep path round the cliffs and I remember — I think I do — the *pretending*, the stress of making these outings bearable. We acted a story of enjoyment: ***The legendary birthplace of King Arthur...*** *This castle was built at least* *500 years after a real or fictitious "Arthur" fought the Sax-*

ons away to the East. In 1978, in the week we returned as a depleted family, we struggled through a real or fictitious "holiday." We pretended to believe in it, even if we didn't, and tried to diminish Nicky's death into an event that happened to him but not to any of the rest of us. The task of making 18th August 1978 a forgettable date, ridiculous though that sounds, was off to a determined start.

Some episodes of the day I can never re-create. So I invent them, knowing it's impossible to invent from nothing. I do the best I can. I sit in the conservatory of my Port Isaac bed-and-breakfast while imagining a 1978 breakfast at The Mill. We squabble over the cornflakes, and Nicky grabs the box from my hand. As he eats, head low to the bowl, a spot of milk settles on his upper lip and his eyes dart sideways to check he can reach the sugar.

In the seat by the window Tim runs his finger down the columns of August tides. We're not in a hurry, but if we miss low tide we'll lose the best of the sand. In the kitchen Mum butters rolls for the picnic, adds the ham, while upstairs Dad tries on his shorts for the first time since August '77. He checks the weather by nudging the curtain aside, and the sun is bright in the sky. He'll be glad to get out, find the wide-open spaces where the boys can let off steam.

Three on the backseat of the Viva and two in the boot. Or Nicky and Jem with Gran and Grandpa, which is good, because then the big boys can stick together. I'd like to impress Guy, the Captain of the School.

I decide to reenact the drive, alone, starting at The Mill. On the way down, into the field, over the cattle grids, onto the concrete tireway and then the final section of metaled lane, I'm newly arrived from Swanage, I'm silent back from the drowning, I'm here in the car again the week after, wishing I were anywhere else, the past within the past within the past.

I turn the car and sit facing the way I came, hoping Jim and Bertie don't pop out to say hello. I've worked through the timings. I contacted the Head of Tides at the UK Hydrographic Office, and from the historical data he can tell me that low tide at Tregardock on 18th August 1978 was 12:05. The next high tide was 5:08 p.m.

When Ted Childs arrived in the lifeboat, he encountered "high water," which I took to mean the tide was more in than out. The beach at Tregardock had disappeared, and from watching the beach closely I know the sand is covered about an hour and forty minutes after each day's low tide. So, on the day in question, the lifeboat arrived sometime after 1:45.

We weren't first-timers at the beach. Watch the tide closely and about forty minutes before the beach fully submerges is the time to think of packing up, and to head for the steps in the rocks. Thirty minutes and we should really be moving, so by my calculations the last swim was probably with fifty minutes of beach remaining, therefore about 1:00. Even if the lifeboat covered the distance from Port Isaac in the shortest possible time (twenty minutes to raise the alarm with Mrs. Thom, twenty minutes to mobilize), Ted would have encountered high water on arrival.

Nicky therefore died between about 1:00 and 1:20 on 18th August 1978. The date was only the start. I can recover the actual time.

Which means we set out from The Mill after breakfast, at about 9.30, to make the most of the daylight hours in which Tregardock is the finest secret beach in Cornwall. Right, then, everyone aboard? We can go. Dad drives carefully, of course he does, he has unsecured kids in the back, and half an eye on his own father who is following in the burgundy Triumph Dolomite. I time the journey: twenty minutes and twenty-seven seconds from The Mill to the beach, on average. Estimated arrival time 9.50.

Slide the car close in to the hedge, on the right of the lane to keep the farm access clear, then the boys tumble out on the left. At the speed of a six-year-old (though I haven't yet timed this with one) the walk down to the beach takes about twenty-three minutes. That's from the end of the lane to the orange life buoy above the steps in the rocks.

"Isn't this wonderful?" Dad says, on 18th August, because the family is reunited and this is genuinely a wonderful way to spend a summer's day; he says it the next time too, a week later. What else is he going to say, now that we're back? The follow-up visit in 1978, after Nicky has been buried in Liddington, is like a blanket over the original event. The shape remains, but none of the detail. I want to remove the smother of the blanket, but to study the blanket too.

Down the steps in the solid rock (careful!), over loose boulders then rock pools then sand, wet acres of the stuff offered up by the retreating tide. On the beach I walk back and forth, waiting for the tidal equivalent of 1:00. I've worked out that the full reappearance of 1978's precise circumstances depends on replicating the exact state of the tide.

Before then, find the location of our camp while the tide is out. I walk to the left, far enough to feel distanced from anyone else, then a little farther. I can't find the place. I take out the paper wallet of last-day photos and hold them up against the landscape. I try to match reality to the images. Close one eye, open one eye. I can map where we played cricket, the rocky backdrop in the photograph and in life unchanged. I give up on the camp, but measure out a cricket pitch, marking a crease with my toe, then stand at square leg and field to Nicky's batting. Now I do this. Then I did this.

"Come on, Dad," I say, to no one in particular. "Finish him off, put Hake on to bowl."

I hold up another photo against its real-life background, of Tim and Guy and Mum splashing in the water. They're much farther to the right along the beach than I'd remembered.

As for the camp, I have a photo of Gran sitting on blankets, with a rock behind her, but I can't find a match. I go over and over the ground, from one end of the beach to the other. How much change can have taken place? I make allowances for rockfalls, mussel colonies, the arbitrary lay of seaweed and miniature limpets that turn black rock brown.

Tregardock is more variable than I'd imagined. I need to factor in the weather, the angle and height of the sun and the strength and direction of the wind. There's an ancient saying that no man can step in the same river twice—the river changes and so does the man. A similar truth applies to the ocean and shore on a wild Cornish beach. I can't just turn up at Tregardock and expect the past to fall into place. Each time I come, though, I'm better prepared, calculating when the time and tides are right, hoping for a perfect facsimile of the landscape and a revelation of exactly how, and possibly why, the drowning could happen. No doubts will remain in my mind.

I try different seasons. Glasses on, glasses off. I fear I'll never be certain that conditions now are as close as possible to conditions then, and I take this instinct to my friend Dru, once of the merchant marine. She confirms what I've started to suspect: a new moon, as on 18th August 1978, occurs on the same day every nineteen years, but the tides are unlikely to coincide: *the concurrence of lunar phase and tide time will prove so rare as to be effectively none.* This means that at the right time of day, about one in the

afternoon, today's tide conditions will rarely if ever repli-
cate those I can't precisely recall from 1978. I check with
the Hydrographic Office. They agree with Dru.

Doubt breeds more doubt. At Tregardock conditions
are capricious, so I can never say for certain exactly where
we entered the water, and whenever I try to pin down the
place I face a countdown: the beach is fast disappearing. I
look around and all the footprints in the sand are mine,
like a chaotic marching band going over and over the same
piece of ground.

The attic, the interviews, the letters, the driving, my
own books, the United Kingdom Hydrographic Office. I
have been assiduously playing and replaying the story, as if
in some version it might end happily, or at least differently.
My sad story of two small boys in the sea—one survives,
one dies—is not the story I would like to have told.

Then one day research and reality come together. I find
the camp. I have the shape of the rocks behind Gran's head
imprinted on my mind from the photos, and I'm at the
beach at the right time after investigating the tides. I
missed the camp previously because the base of the rock
where Gran sat is under water. Tidal action over the years
has scooped out a moat of sand.

This is definitely the place. The camp is closer to the
steps than I expected (onto the beach, turn right). Which
means our patch of sand where we set out for our last swim
is also farther to the right. The story comes together. One
last swim. Come on, Nicky. Straight down from the camp

the main beach is open and safe, boring. I run to the right and round the back of a large rock, to our own special place, the sand I'd scouted earlier. Here, near the northern headland at the right-hand end of Tregardock, the waves *are* bigger. The waves are bigger today, they were bigger then. The beach is still too wide. This is the place, but not yet. The patch of sand will shrink as the tide comes in.

I wait. I watch the swell come at an angle off the headland, waves in from the right, sand dragging out to the left. Crosscurrents, not a familiar danger at the Old Town Gardens in Swindon, where usually we went to play. I stand in the shallows and feel the tide on my feet. I marvel at the undertow, dragging the sand from beneath my toes, but can't see the fun. I wade in deeper, up to my knees, then change my mind. Most days of the year, swimming in these waters isn't recommended. Ask the local RNLI: the lifeboat crews know the route to Tregardock.

Am I frightened a rogue wave will pick me up and sweep me out? I am not; that never happened. I do notice that the camber of the sand is steep here (conspicuous before the tide comes in, then hidden), and there's a kind of hump just at the wrong place, which will accelerate the deepening of the water. Easy to see the risks, at this stage of the tide, now that I bother to look. Back then, our timing was simply unlucky. I should acknowledge the senseless chain of events — nothing but timidity would have saved us.

We were not afraid. Summer holiday, beach, last swim, waves, adventure. We plowed straight in.

Not yet, the tide isn't quite there, but soon it will be, sooner than you'd expect. Mum is packing the lunch after the best of the day. Four of us had traveled long-distance by car on the 17th, and we'd been cavorting at Tregardock since the tide was halfway out at ten that morning, three hours ago. Everyone is tired, beneath the burning sun.

Along with the ancient rocks, I wait. A rock the size of a cricket scorebox, larger, perfectly obscures my view of the camp, about eighty meters away. I retreat round the back of this rock, then jog out from behind it and onto the little beach, to surprise my memory with a replica of the past. Not yet. The patch of sand is still too big. Soon. There are often freak waves, so as Chris Bolton said, not that freakish at all. These waves can eat up an extra ten meters of beach in one go, but they don't rush in often enough to act as a warning. Back behind the rock, out I trot again, to encounter afresh the beach and the sea and sky. Depending on the timing, the beach can look appealing and innocent. No sign of the more dangerous waves. Good luck, bad luck.

Once we were in, a thrilling freak wave would suddenly have put ten more meters between us and dry land. Taking our bearings from the cliffs to the right, we thought we were in the same place; we were, it was the Atlantic Ocean that had moved.

Now.

I check the time. Matched against high tide on 18th August 1978, the equivalent is 1:13. I have the time we went into the water. Wait. I stand on the shore and endure a sickly, queasy few minutes. As the last person to see Nicky alive — confirmed by Ted Childs — I know how far out we went. I see where we were and, busy with our laughing and jumping, we had no idea the planet was shifting around us. Even on a calm day some of the waves are magnificent. At astonishing speed this part of the beach is closing off, becoming a cove. I sight the full length of Tregardock to my left and yes, the main beach is fine, with plenty of time to spare.

Unlike here. Now. I locate where we were, and the water is about chest-high to an eleven-year-old, and to eyes at sea level the rocks are in the eyeline, forming a cove, making us invisible. Now. Seven minutes after going into the water, at about 1:20, the panic starts. I'd have to be in the water to be absolutely sure, but I'm not going to do that, even so many years later. Nicky's head goes under (1:21). I swim back in (1:22).

My body hollows out, like an undertow dragging away my heart and innards, leaving behind loss, a memory of loss. On the sand I turn to run, and the sea has rushed in so the cliff at the back of the beach is closer than it was, especially if an adult is there. I run to him, let him know a boy's in the water, a boy is in the water. He stands up with manly purpose and hands me his trivial sunglasses. I run again, back toward the family, over sand, over rocks, and the glasses are in my left hand and I smash them onto a rock. I run toward the people I love.

He's in the sea, I tried to save him.

In the natural shelter of the family camp, where in August 1978 we laid blankets beside the rocks, since partially submerged, I bend over and, with my hands on my knees, I sob. The place is in me, the physicality of the memory. Tears drop onto the lenses of my glasses and I bring up huge gulps of undigested grief. Then the sound groaning from my own mouth pulls me up—too low, the bass of a grown man. Wrong. At a time like this a child can cry, a child should be crying now.

I straighten up. I don't trust the grief breaking out from inside me to last. I run back to the big rock, reenacting the excitement from before the swimming, round the rock to the beach, the sea, look at the amazing waves! Immediately I reach the water I turn round, rerun in my own footprints back to the man at the cliff, take his glasses, leap over rock and sand and smash the sunglasses and hare back fast to camp.

The same story. I reenact the movements to prompt a revelation, and when the emotion surges the acting comes to an end. I can't help myself. I buckle over, hands on knees, and sob out loud. "I tried, I tried," bawled out to no one, nobody here but me. Something must be done, but I don't know what. I heave out blunt pebbles of semi-eroded grief. I hear a man crying. Wrong, not the sound I'm expecting to hear. I straighten up. I escape myself, into an imagining of what happened next.

I visualize the kerfuffle in our sheltered camp, the shouting, the dramatic scene. Dad would have hated that, the fuss, wherever he was. From my mum a *Colin!* Gran in shock, *I'll fetch the others.* And I wail. I am wailing, and I am telling lies.

"I tried, I tried."

These are the lost words that come back to me with the tears, at the end of the line that is now.

Already, Dad is clambering over the rocks, bashing and grazing his shins. Someone decides the children shouldn't see this. Maybe it was him, his first reaction. I don't know. I don't know my own father. But we were the first to leave, and we'd almost reached the lane before help arrived thirty, forty minutes too late.

I walk slowly toward the steps, negotiate the rock pools and loose boulders, climb the deep indentations in the rock. On the grass beside the life buoy I stop and look back, down. This is where Mum waited, clutching Nicky's shoe to her throat and not being comforted by well-intentioned strangers. Where is the lifeboat? Where is the rescue helicopter?

From up here I see the scorebox rock already surrounded by white water, and beyond that a backbone of smaller rocks reaching into the sea to confirm my memory of a cove. If Dad sliced up his legs on the last rock along, by my calculations he'd have been twenty meters from Nicky, at the most. The water was calm, Ted Childs of the RNLI (headmaster) says so. On the calmer days at Tregardock it is never inconceivable to jump into the ocean to save the life of a child.

Jump, Dad. Leap in and have a go. Do your best. Try your hardest, then keep trying.

Maybe his failure to jump explains his later silence, and why he made questions feel unwelcome. Emotional endurance can be brave, we know that in our family, but pushing on regardless is not the only form bravery takes. Up here where rock gives way to grass, I can see that Nicky died while the marked-out crease for cricket was still intact on the main expanse of sand. From up here, from down there, from every angle, his death feels avoidable. None of the stories I tell make sense of it.

I take the hard walk up to the car with head lowered, legs heavy and arms hanging loose (21 minutes 18 seconds). Endurance is not the same as courage, not always.

The accident happened earlier in the day than I'd have thought, and the lifeboat was a long time too late (high water at 1:48 is twenty-eight minutes after we first started to struggle). Nicky was dead by then; he'd been dead for a while, and so the charade began. I knew but didn't dare say. Dad had scrambled out to within twenty meters. He watched Ted pull Nicky from the water, and he watched his limp dead son rise, dripping, with the winchman into the belly of the Wessex.

He must have known, like I knew. As he followed by road in the coast-guard Land Rover he knew his son was dead, and at last I've found a connection between us. We're a pair of lying, hopeful bastards. We knew before the others, and we hid our knowledge. We pretended everything might turn out fine, then pushed the truth out of sight and endured.

I drive north along the coastal road to Bude. As a representative of HM Coastguard, I imagine I would observe the speed limits. No need for flashing lights, for drama. The desperate parents in the back want me to get there quickly, but they shouldn't be in such a hurry. With all my coast-guard experience, I know too.

The hospital is a long single-story building—the helicopter either has to land in the car park or across town at the rugby club. The doctor on duty that day has time to compose himself before the parents arrive, as does the senior nursing sister. Neither of them would volunteer to break the news.

I drive south again toward Port Isaac. Through the outskirts of Bude my chest fills with the sense of having left something behind, something important, not at the hospital but at the beach. I hurry back to Tregardock, to find whatever it is I've lost. I walk down the path, through the opening in the cliffs, but arrive too late. The beach is nowhere to be seen, replaced by the heave of the implacable Atlantic. I've done my best, but whatever I lost or left behind, I'm not going to find it now.

I think a life can have a center, which earlier and later experiences will never match. This could be a triumph, but perhaps more commonly it's a trauma, and if not the center, then this event provides a center of gravity. Mine is at

Tregardock, and lasts from 18th August 1978 until the end of the week following the funeral, when back in Cornwall we acted as if accidents never happen. Whatever I went looking for on that first day in the graveyard at Liddington, this is what I found: the extra week, the one we'd blacked out of existence.

The decision to drive straight from the funeral back to The Mill was a fantastic gesture of defiance. Death was not going to ruin an English family holiday, and after all these years I feel the stubborn effort of our pretense. Tregardock is "just" a beach, and the Atlantic Ocean "just" the sea, and our return trip to Cornwall no more than a week we're due because we booked and paid in advance. Grief is an inconvenience, just an emotion and therefore subordinate to strength of will.

I bet we set up our camp in a different place, though, way over to the left in the vast safety of open sand. No wonder I looked there first for the camp, because that's where it was, a week too late.

We deleted the memory, and the extra week remained as a barrier, intact until now and separating us from the emotional impact of Nicky's drowning. Our forced, forgotten smiles provided a template for underestimating emotion, but his death happened to all of us, not just to him. I've tried to locate and live the grief, to reanimate the shock of the day. That has been the aim of the inquest, the end of the pretense: we can't have the same holiday in the same place without Nicky, we can't live an uninterrupted life.

Since the age of eleven I've dodged the pain, generally kept feeling to a minimum as a precaution against sudden disaster. I've sleepwalked through pre-forgotten days. The project was *not* to feel, as encouraged in that extra week, until, hard of heart, I can ask a seventy-five-year-old retired headmaster to describe pulling a small drowned boy from the sea, when that dead boy is my brother. And I don't even blink. Ted, tell me, how did it feel? I lean in very close toward him, to watch the tears as they form in his yellow-and-pale-blue eyes.

Smart, savage, I'm as competitive and wary as an eleven-year-old, and my interests haven't changed: cricket, reading, coming top of the class. I like daydreaming and feeling sorry for myself and not being punished. I avoid squits who cry. I have stalled at 1978, as did Nicky.

I'd like to grow up, but I don't want to leave Nicky behind, again. In his Letts Schoolboys' Diary 1978, Nicky records his height as four feet and his weight as fifty-two pounds. He's a small boy, and from my own sons I know how objectively small that is. But in my mind he's not small—he's still only two years younger than I am.

Once, just the once while writing this book, after a dream about waterboarding my mum, I dreamed him. He was standing beside a bus. He hadn't grown up, and may have been eight, anyway younger than nine. He smiled at me; we were immensely pleased to see each other. I went up to him, I made the move, and we were thrilled to be reunited. We started running. We sprinted side by side up an English street, away from the bus and from other dreams. I was so happy I cried.

I miss him as an adult, the Nicky who never became a Nick. A solid, grown-up Nick Beard, on his laminated name badge at the induction day for a new job. A sporting Bearders, phoning round in search of a fellow opening bowler. N. P. Beard, the signature on his divorce papers.

The paper and cloth remnants of his short life are scattered across the floor of my room, fragments of Nicky stopping at 1978. *I only hope that you will come to believe that there must be a reason for the little chap being taken. He must have brought great happiness during his short life which can never be lost.* I've been through the evidence and haven't found a reason.

My education (the early mornings, the short trousers, the Latin) promised that whoever answered the difficult questions would move to the top of the class. Why were Nicky and I playing together, at that particular time, and why did we run away from the others? How did we come to ignore the fears and inland caution of Middle England? What caused the death of Nicholas Beard (9)?

I came first in a class of twelve boys.

Nicky's life and death is not a story with an answer, or a resolution. What I have is my inquest, and the relics of Nicky's real existence carefully curated as if into a shiny red case, to be stored with love in an attic. I don't believe the original red case existed, except as a longed-for treasure chest of stuff worth keeping. If only we hadn't been so successful at forgetting. The red case, a fiction, stood in for all that was lost.

As a final constructive gesture, I buy a red Mossman thirty-six-inch steamer trunk, an expensive piece of secure luggage in which to store the balance of Nicky's lifetime. The box is 36 × 20 × 16 inches, taller but shorter than a small coffin, with space to spare, should further items of Nicky's come to light. I put in the stack of card-covered schoolbooks, about a foot high; I find room for box-files containing the correspondence, the school reports, and the newspaper cuttings. I put in the cricket scorebook and the unused name tapes, the photos and boxes of slides.

I cover Nicky's belongings with his blazer and the tracksuit top, then his school cap and his blue cricket hat. Finally, I put in the manuscript of this book, and close the lid. This is Nicky, his life and his death, as far as we can know.

Acknowledgments

This book could not have been written without the support, time, and generosity of my mum, Felicity Beard, and my brothers Tim and Jem. I will be forever grateful to all three of them for sharing my feeling that the time had come to talk about Nicky.

For bringing information about a 1970s schooling to light, it was a pleasure to be reacquainted with Chris Field and Henry Boddington, both formerly of Pinewood School. I'm also indebted to Guy Hake for his memories of the day itself.

In Cornwall, Bertie and Jim Watson at The Mill were forgiving of an unsolicited approach from a stranger, and kindly invited me into their home.

The RNLI has been consistently helpful throughout the writing of this book, initially through Karen Harris of the RNLI archive in Poole, then directly at the RNLI Port Isaac Lifeboat Station. In particular at Port Isaac, I'd like to thank Chris Bolton, Bob Bulgin, and of course Ted Childs.

I was able to retrieve valuable documentary evidence thanks to the conscientious record-keeping of Hillier Funeral Service in Swindon, the Cornwall Coroner in Truro, the Head of Tides at the United Kingdom Hydrographic Office, and the Newsroom of the British Library in London.

Finally, this book was greatly improved by the expert yet sensitive input of my outstanding editor Stuart Williams, as well as the consistently wise guidance of my agent Lucy Luck. I thank them both for their unwavering support.

About the Author

Richard Beard's six novels include *Lazarus Is Dead*, *Dry Bones*, and *Damascus*, which was a *New York Times* Notable Book of the Year. In the UK, he has been short-listed for the BBC National Short Story Award and long-listed for the Sunday *Times* EFG Private Bank Short Story Award. His latest novel *Acts of the Assassins* was short-listed for the Goldsmiths Prize in 2015. He is also the author of four books of narrative nonfiction. Formerly director of the National Academy of Writing in London, he was a visiting professor (2016–17) at the University of Tokyo, and has a creative writing fellowship at the University of East Anglia.